THE
VOICE OF
HEBREWS

THE MYSTERY OF MĒL-KĬZ'Ĕ-DĔK

Retold by
Greg Garrett

with

Commentary by
David B. Capes

A SCRIPTURE PROJECT TO REDISCOVER ⌐⌐⌐⌐ OF THE BIBLE

THOMAS NE
Since 1798

NASHVILLE   DALLAS   MEXICO CITY   RIO DE JANEIRO   BEIJING

CONTRIBUTORS

The Voice of Hebrews: *The Mystery of Melchizedek*

SCRIPTURES RETOLD BY: Greg Garrett

COMMENTARY BY:
David B. Capes

SCHOLARLY REVIEW BY:
David B. Capes
Peter H. Davids

EDITORIAL REVIEW BY:
Chris Seay
James F. Couch, Jr.
Maleah Bell
Marilyn Duncan
Amanda Haley
Kelly Hall
Merrie Noland

A SCRIPTURE PROJECT TO REDISCOVER THE STORY OF THE BIBLE

TABLE OF CONTENTS

Section Three // **Other products from** the voice™

PREFACE

the voice.
A Scripture project to rediscover the story of the Bible

Any literary project reflects the age in which it is written. **The Voice** is created for and by a church in great transition. Throughout the body of Christ, extensive discussions are ongoing about a variety of issues including style of worship, how we separate culture from our theology, and what is essential truth. In fact, we are struggling with what is truth. At the center of this discussion is the role of Scripture. This discussion is heating up with strong words being exchanged. Instead of furthering the division over culture and theology, it is time to bring the body of Christ together again around the Bible. Thomas Nelson Publishers and Ecclesia Bible Society together are developing Scripture products that foster spiritual growth and theological exploration out of a heart for worship and mission. We have dedicated ourselves to hearing and proclaiming God's voice through this project.

Previously most Bibles and biblical reference works were produced by professional scholars writing in academic settings. **The Voice** uniquely represents collaboration among scholars, pastors, writers, musicians, poets, and other artists. The goal is to create the finest Bible products to help believers experience the joy and wonder of God's revelation. Four key words describe the vision of this project:

- holistic // considers heart, soul, and mind
- beautiful // achieves literary and artistic excellence
- sensitive // respects cultural shifts and the need for accuracy
- balanced // includes theologically diverse writers and scholars

Uniqueness of *The Voice*

About 40 different human authors are believed to have been inspired by God to write the Scriptures. **The Voice** retains the perspective of the human writers. Most English translations attempt to even out the styles of the different authors in sentence structure and vocabulary. Instead, **The Voice** distinguishes the uniqueness of each author. The heart of the project is retelling the story of the Bible in a form as fluid as modern literary works yet remaining true to the original manuscripts. First, accomplished writers create an English rendering; then, respected Bible scholars adjust the rendering to align the manuscript with the original texts. Attention is paid to the use of idioms, artistic elements, confusion of pronouns, repetition of conjunctives, modern sentence structure, and the public reading of the passage. In the process, the writer or scholar may adjust the arrangement of words or expand the phrasing to create an English equivalent.

To help the reader understand how the new rendering of a passage compares to the original manuscripts, several indicators are imbedded within the text. Italic type indicates words not directly tied to a dynamic translation of the original language. Material delineated by a screened box expands on the theme. This portion is not taken directly from the original language. To avoid the endless repetition of simple conjunctives, dialog is formatted as a screenplay. The speaker is indicated, the dialog is indented, and quotation marks are not used. This helps greatly in the public reading of Scripture. Sometimes the original text includes interruptions in the dialog to indicate attitude of the speaker or who is being spoken to. This is shown either as a stage direction immediately following the speaker's name or as part of the narrative section that immediately precedes the speaker's name. The screenplay format clearly shows who is speaking.

Throughout *The Voice,* other language devices improve readability. We follow the standard conventions used in most translations regarding textual evidence. *The Voice* is based on the earliest and best manuscripts from the original languages (Greek, Hebrew, and Aramaic). When significant variations influence a reading, we follow the publishing standard by bracketing the passage and placing a note at the bottom of the page while maintaining the traditional chapter and verse divisions. The footnotes reference quoted material and help the reader understand the translation for a particular word. Words that are borrowed from another language or words that are not common outside of the theological community (such as baptism, repentance, and salvation) are translated into more common terminology. For clarity, some pronouns are replaced with their antecedents. Word order and parts of speech are sometimes altered to help the reader understand the original passage.

— Ecclesia Bible Society

ABOUT *THE VOICE* PROJECT

As retold, edited, and illustrated by a gifted team
of writers, scholars, poets, and storytellers

A New Way to Process Ideas

Chris Seay's (president of Ecclesia Bible Society) vision for **The Voice** goes
back 15 years to his early attempts to teach the Bible in the narrative as the
story of God. As Western culture has moved into what is now referred to as
postmodernism, Chris observed that the way a new generation processes
ideas and information raises obstacles to traditional methods of teaching
biblical content. His desire has grown to present the Bible in ways that over-
come these obstacles to people coming to faith. Instead of propositional-
based thought patterns, people today are more likely to interact with events
and individuals through complex observations involving emotions, cognitive
processes, tactile experiences, and spiritual awareness. Much as in the para-
bles of Jesus and in the metaphors of the prophets, narrative communication
touches the whole person.

Hence, out of that early vision comes the need in a postmodern culture
to present Scripture in a narrative form. The result is a retelling of the
Scriptures: **The Voice**, not of words, but of meaning and experience.

The Timeless Narrative

The Voice is a fresh expression of the timeless narrative known as the Bible.
Stories that were told to emerging generations of God's goodness by their
grandparents and tribal leaders were recorded and assembled to form the
Christian Scriptures. Too often, the passion, grit, humor, and beauty has been
lost in the translation process. **The Voice** seeks to recapture what was lost.

From these early explorations by Chris and others has come **The Voice**: a
Scripture project to rediscover the story of the Bible. Thomas Nelson
Publishers and Ecclesia Bible Society have joined together to stimulate
unique creative experiences and to develop Scripture products and resources
to foster spiritual growth and theological exploration out of a heart for the
mission of the church and worship of God.

Traditional Translations

Putting the Bible into the language of modern readers has too often been a painstaking process of correlating the biblical languages to the English vernacular. The Bible is filled with passages intended to inspire, captivate, and depict beauty. The old school of translation most often fails at attempts to communicate beauty, poetry, and story. *The Voice* is a collage of compelling narratives, poetry, song, truth, and wisdom. *The Voice* will call you to enter into the whole story of God with your heart, soul, and mind.

A New Retelling

One way to describe this approach is to say that it is a "soul translation," not just a "mind translation." But "translation" is not the right word. It is really the retelling of the story. The "retelling" involves translation and paraphrase, but mostly entering into the story of the Scriptures and recreating the event for our culture and time. It doesn't ignore the role of scholars, but it also values the role of writers, poets, songwriters, and artists. Instead, a team of scholars partner with a writer to blend the mood and voice of the original author with an accurate rendering of words of the text in English.

    The Voice is unique in that it represents collaboration among scholars, writers, musicians, and other artists. Its goal is to create the finest Bible products to help believers experience the joy and wonder of God's revelation. In this time of great transition within the church, we are seeking to give gifted individuals opportunities to craft a variety of products and experiences: a translation of the Scriptures, worship music, worship film festivals, biblical art, worship conferences, gatherings of creative thinkers, a Web site for individuals and churches to share biblical resources, and books derived from exploration during the Bible translation work.

    The heart of each product within *The Voice* project is the retelling of the Bible story. To accomplish the objectives of the project and to facilitate the various products envisioned within the project, the Bible text is being translated. We trust that this retelling will be a helpful contribution to a fresh engagement with Scripture. The Bible is the greatest story ever told, but it often doesn't read like it. *The Voice* brings the biblical narratives to life and reads more like a great novel than the traditional versions of the Bible that are seldom opened in contemporary culture.

Readable and Enjoyable

A careful process is being followed to assure that the spiritual, emotional, and artistic goals of the project are met. First, the retelling of the Bible has been designed to be readable and enjoyable by emphasizing the narrative nature of Scripture. Beyond simply providing a set of accurately translated individual words, phrases, and sentences, our teams were charged to render the biblical texts with sensitivity to the flow of the unfolding story. We asked them to see themselves not only as guardians of the sacred text, but also as storytellers, because we believe that the Bible has always been intended to be heard as the sacred story of the people of God. We assigned each literary unit (for example, the writings of John or Paul) to a team that included a skilled writer and biblical and theological scholars, seeking to achieve a mixture of scholarly expertise and literary skill.

Personal and Diverse

Second, as a consequence of this team approach, *The Voice* is both personal and diverse. God used about 40 human instruments to communicate His message, and each one has a unique voice or literary style. Standard translations tend to flatten these individual styles so that each book reads more or less like the others—with a kind of impersonal textbook-style prose. Some translations and paraphrases have paid more attention to literary style—but again, the literary style of one writer, no matter how gifted, can unintentionally obscure the diversity of the original voices. To address these problems, we asked our teams to try to feel and convey the diverse literary styles of the original authors.

Faithful

Third, we have taken care that *The Voice* is faithful and that it avoids prejudice. Anyone who has worked with translation and paraphrase knows that there is no such thing as a completely unbiased or objective translation. So, while we do not pretend to be purely objective, we asked our teams to seek to be as faithful as possible to the biblical message as they understood it together. In addition, as we partnered biblical scholars and theologians with our writers, we intentionally built teams that did not share any single theological tradition. Their diversity has helped each of them not to be trapped within his or her own individual preconceptions, resulting in a faithful and fresh rendering of the Bible.

Stimulating and Creative

Fourth, we have worked hard to make *The Voice* both stimulating and creative. As we engaged the biblical text, we realized again and again that certain terms have conventional associations for modern readers that would not have been present for the original readers—and that the original readers would have been struck by certain things that remain invisible or opaque to modern readers. Even more, we realized that modern readers from different religious or cultural traditions would hear the same words differently. For example, when Roman Catholic or Eastern Orthodox readers encounter the word "baptism," a very different set of meanings and associations come to mind than those that would arise in the minds of Baptist or Pentecostal readers. And a secular person encountering the text would have still different associations. The situation is made even more complex when we realize that *none* of these associations may resemble the ones that would have come to mind when John invited Jewish peasants and Pharisees into the water of the Jordan River in the months before Jesus began His public ministry. It is far harder than most people realize to help today's readers recapture the original impact of a single word like "baptism." In light of this challenge, we decided, whenever possible, to select words that would stimulate fresh thinking rather than reinforce unexamined assumptions. We want the next generation of Bible readers—whatever their background—to have the best opportunity possible to hear God's message the way the first generation of Bible readers heard it.

Transformative

Finally, we desire that this translation will be useful and transformative. It is all too common in many of our Protestant churches to have only a few verses of biblical text read in a service, and then that selection too often becomes a jumping-off point for a sermon that is at best peripherally related to, much less rooted in, the Bible itself. The goal of *The Voice* is to promote the public reading of longer sections of Scripture—followed by thoughtful engagement with the biblical narrative in its richness and fullness and dramatic flow. We believe the Bible itself, in all its diversity and energy and dynamism, is the message; it is not merely the jumping-off point.

The various creations of the project bring creative application of commentary and interpretive tools. These are clearly indicated and separated from the Bible text that is drawn directly from traditional sources. Along with the creative resources and fresh expressions of God's Word, the reader has the benefit of centuries of biblical research applied dynamically to our rapidly changing culture.

The products underway in **The Voice** include dynamic and interactive presentations of the critical passages in the life of Jesus and the early church, recorded musical presentation of Scripture originally used in worship or uniquely structured for worship, artwork commissioned from young artists, dramatized audio presentations from the Gospels and the Old Testament historical books, film commentary on our society using the words of Scripture, and exploration of the voice of each human author of the Bible.

The first product for **The Voice**, entitled *The Last Eyewitness: The Final Week*, released Spring 2006, follows Jesus through His final week of life on earth through the firsthand account of John the apostle. This book combines the drama of the text with the artwork of Rob Pepper into a captivating retelling of Jesus' final days. The second product, *The Dust Off Their Feet: Lessons from the First Church*, was released September 2006 and includes the entire Book of Acts retold by Brian McLaren with commentary and articles written by nine scholars and pastors. *The Voice of Matthew* was released January 2007 with the Gospel of Matthew retold by Lauren Winner including Lauren's devotional commentary, along with cultural and historical notes. *The Voice of Luke: Not Even Sandals,* released June 2007, contains the Gospel of Luke retold by Brian McLaren and includes his devotional notes.

The Voice from on High, published in the fall of 2007, contains over 700 verses from 19 Old Testament and New Testament books. The story of the Liberating King is shown to run through the Bible from Genesis to Revelation. Over a dozen writers have contributed to the retelling of the Scriptures with reflections by Jonathan Hal Reynolds. *The Voice Revealed* is the full Gospel of John retold by Chris Seay in a compact edition to introduce others to the faith. *The Voice of Mark* retold by Greg Garrett with commentary by Matthew Paul Turner will complete the products for the winter, and *The Voice of Romans* will be published Summer, 2008.

The Team

The team writing **The Voice** brings unprecedented gifts to this unique project. An award-winning fiction writer, an acclaimed poet, a pastor renowned for using art and narrative in his preaching and teaching, Greek and Hebrew authorities, and biblical scholars are all coming together to capture the beauty and diversity of God's Word.

Writers

The contributors to *The Voice of Hebrews: The Mystery of Melchizedek* are:

• Greg Garrett—Professor of English at Baylor University and writer in residence at the Episcopal Theological Seminary of the Southwest. He is the author of the critically acclaimed novels *Free Bird* and *Cycling*, the memoir *Crossing Myself*, and nonfiction books, including *The Gospel Reloaded* (with Chris Seay) and *The Gospel According to Hollywood*.

• David B. Capes, PhD— Professor of Greek and New Testament at Houston Baptist University. He has written several books, including *The Last Eyewitness: the Final Week, Rediscovering Paul,* and *The Footsteps of Jesus in the Holy Land.* Dr. Capes also served as a critical reviewer for the text of Hebrews,

along with

• Peter H. Davids, PhD—Adjunct Professor at Tyndale Theological Amsterdam, International Teams Innsbrook, and resident scholar at Basileia Vineyard Bern. He is the author of commentaries on the books of James, 1 & 2 Peter, and Jude and is the editor of the *Dictionary of Late New Testament and Its Development*.

The writers for ***The Voice*** include:

Eric Bryant—pastor/author
David B. Capes—professor/author
Don Chaffer—singer/songwriter/poet
Lori Chaffer—singer/songwriter/poet
Tara Leigh Cobble—singer/songwriter
Robert Creech—pastor/author
Greg Garrett—professor/author
Christena Graves—singer
Sara Groves—singer/songwriter

Amanda Haley—archaeology scholar/editor

Charlie Hall—singer/songwriter

Kelly Hall—editor/poet

Greg Holder—pastor

Justin Hyde—pastor/author

Andrew Jones—pastor/consultant

E. Chad Karger—counselor/author/pastor

Tim Keel—pastor

Greg LaFollette—musician/songwriter

Evan Lauer—pastor/author

Phuc Luu—chaplain/adjunct instructor

Christian McCabe—pastor/artist

Brian McLaren—pastor/author

Donald Miller—author

Sean Palmer—pastor

Jonathan Hal Reynolds—poet

Chris Seay—pastor/author

Robbie Seay—singer/songwriter

Kerry Shook—pastor

Chuck Smith, Jr.—pastor/author

Allison Smythe—poet

Leonard Sweet—author

Kristin Swenson—professor/author

Alison Thomas—speaker/apologist

Phyllis Tickle—author

Matthew Paul Turner—author/speaker

Lauren Winner—lecturer/author

Seth Woods—singer/songwriter

Dieter Zander—pastor/author

Scholars

Biblical and theological scholars for *The Voice* include:

Joseph Blair, ThD—professor

Darrell L. Bock, PhD—professor

David B. Capes, PhD—author/professor, HBU

Alan Culpepper, PhD—dean/professor
Peter H. Davids, PhD—pastor/professor
J. Andrew Dearman, PhD—professor
J. R. Dodson, MDiv—adjunct professor
Brett Dutton, PhD—pastor/adjunct professor
Dave Garber, PhD—professor
Mark Gignilliat, PhD—assistant professor
Peter Rhea Jones, Sr., PhD—pastor/professor
Sheri Klouda, PhD—professor
Tremper Longman, PhD—professor
Creig Marlowe, PhD—dean/professor
Troy Miller, PhD—professor
Frank Patrick—assistant professor
Chuck Pitts, PhD—professor
Brian Russell, PhD—associate professor
Nancy de Claissé Walford, PhD—professor
Kenneth Waters, Sr., PhD—professor
Jack Wisdom, JD—lawyer

A WORD ABOUT THIS BOOK ...

I am not exaggerating when I say I love the Bible. It sounds like I'm being overly spiritual, trying to impress my old Sunday School teachers, or playing teacher's pet to the Creator of the heavens and the earth. But I am definitely not overly spiritual or overtly pious; I am just a man struggling to enjoy the beauty God created and trying to love others as much as I already love myself. The truth is that the story of God as revealed through the Bible has shaped my life in strong and mysterious ways. If not for the truth in its pages, my life would be a mess.

I have been a follower of Christ for 30 years and a pastor expected to stand in the pulpit (or, in my case, next to the stool) and preach the Bible every week for 18 years. I have spent countless hours reading, studying, and teaching the Bible; and what I find in its pages never ceases to amaze me. Its wisdom is the answer when my life demands profound truth, and its words are filled with tenderness and discipline when I need the touch of a loving parent. If I have decisions to make, whether large or small, I read the Bible. I don't scour it expecting the answer to be written in black and white—although sometimes it is—but I do know that as my heart centers in the truth, the world looks different to me.

I cannot imagine being an early Christian who did not have this complete Christian canon. The Bible is a source of wisdom, history, inspiration, comfort, and prayers. Yet millions of Christians lived in a time when they could not even imagine the Bible as we know it; and for centuries after that, most were incapable of reading the newly formed canon. What did they do when they needed to hear God's wisdom and surround themselves with His truth? They did not have all the Gospels and likely never saw more than one letter written by the emissary Paul. For many, the only link between the Judaism they once knew and the fulfillment of the Scriptures through Jesus the long-awaited Liberating King was this document we call Hebrews. It was the piece of literature that knit the past to the future by explaining liberation through Jesus, who was not recognized as the Liberating King by many Hebrews. It was a fusion, if you will, of the stories of the Hebrew Scriptures and the teachings of Jesus and His kingdom.

Hebrews is a unique book that I appreciate now more than ever. David Capes and Greg Garrett are two of the brightest and most creative people I know, and the partnership between a biblical scholar (David) and a novelist (Greg) allows the mysteries in Hebrews to be explored with a great imagination that is grounded in historical truth. It is filled with mysteries to be discovered, wisdom that is easily mined, and a focus on Jesus the Liberating King that will call everyone to lay down their own lives and take up their own crosses. So sit back, allow your imagination to guide you through a book cherished by early followers of the Liberator, and pray that we will continue to live into this same story that continues to this day. Blessings!

Chris Seay
President, Ecclesia Bible Society

Section One // **The Book of Hebrews**

INTRODUCTION

The letter to the Hebrews quotes from and alludes to a collection of 39 books (known today as the Old Testament) more than any other New Testament writing. The reason is simple: this collection of Hebrew Scriptures is the Bible for the earliest followers of Jesus, the ones who are reading this letter. It is in these 39 books that the first-century Jewish Christians hear the voice of God, so our writer appeals to the Scriptures' authority to proclaim that Jesus the Liberating King is the final, full, and definitive revelation of God. These new Christians don't have a New Testament; it is still being written. As we read through the magnificent books of the New Testament, we should never forget that the Bible of Jesus, Peter, Paul, and the early church is the Old Testament.

So what is contained in this Old Testament? At its heart is a narrative of God's covenants with and promises to His people and the world. Concerned with the proliferation of evil, sin, and its dire consequences on His creation, God decides that the best route to reclaim His broken creation is to reveal Himself to one person, and to another, and then to another, on the way to redeeming the entire world. Essentially, the Old Testament tells the story of four covenants that lay the foundation for the new covenant inaugurated in Jesus, our Liberating King.

The first covenant involves God's promise to Noah, his family, and the world that He will never again destroy the earth with a flood. God places a rainbow in the sky as a sign of that promise. When God sees the rainbow, He remembers His covenant. When the floodwaters recede and the ark is back on dry land, He instructs Noah and his family to be fruitful, multiply, and fill the earth, just as He had instructed the first man and woman in the garden. Creation starts over with Noah, Ms. Noah, and their children. Still, it isn't long before sin's presence is felt once again among the new humanity.

God makes a second covenant with Abraham many generations after Noah's descendants have divided into nations and established strange traditions. He promises to give the wandering nomad a land, to make him a great nation, to give him a great name, and, perhaps most significantly, to bless all the nations of the world through his descendants.* Abraham responds to

Genesis 12:1-3

God's call with faith and obedience; but his journey ahead is difficult, and he doesn't see all of God's promises fulfilled in his lifetime. Yet, on his way back from victory in battle, Abraham meets a mysterious person named Melchizedek, the king of Salem.

This puzzling figure seems to appear out of nowhere and fades just as quickly into the dust of history. Is he a man or an angel or something else altogether? As a priest of the Most High God, he receives from Abraham one-tenth of the spoils of battle and blesses him and his children just as God did. If this short story had been all that was ever told or written about Melchizedek, then this mysterious figure might have been lost forever. But his legacy is kept alive in Psalm 110, a royal psalm celebrating the installment of David's son as king and ideal priest according to the "order of Melchizedek." If an order of priests is named for him, then Melchizedek must be much more than a human king during Abraham's life. But more about Melchizedek later in our story.

After Abraham's death, God renews the second covenant with each of his sons, who wrestle with God and struggle to remain faithful. Eventually, Abraham's children sojourn south to Egypt and become slaves in that land under Pharaoh's heel. The promise that Abraham would become a great nation seemed all but impossible.

The third covenant in the Old Testament is between God and Israel, the descendants of Abraham. This covenant begins with a powerful act of deliverance when God rescues the Hebrew slaves from bondage in Egypt. The Eternal One answers the prayers of Abraham's hurting people, raising up Moses to demand from Pharaoh that the Hebrew people be set free. After a convincing display of power over the gods of Egypt and the waters of the sea, God instructs Moses to lead the former slaves to Mount Sinai. There Moses receives God's law, His blueprint for their lives and society. God promises to be with His people, to protect and deliver them, and finally to lead them into the promised land, a land flowing with milk and honey. In this covenant, the people of Israel pledge to obey and worship God alone, or else they will face harsh consequences. While obedience to God is guaranteed to bring blessing, disobedience brings adversity and ultimately exile from that land of promise.

Centuries later, God speaks to King David through the prophet Nathan, making a fourth covenant. God promises David three things: David's son will build God a temple, his dynasty will continue forever, and God will relate to David's son as His own.* God's covenant with David becomes the basis for the expectation that one day David's son would be the Liberating King. According to the prophets, the Liberating King would be God's agent to realize all of God's promises, to renew the world, and to bring salvation to the ends of the earth.

These covenant relationships comprise the story of God's dealings with the world, His people, and ultimately all the nations. As God's plan and will unfold, each covenant brings the world nearer to God's kingdom, His ultimate rule over creation. Although the word "testament" can mean "covenant," the Old Testament tells the story of God's multiple covenants with multiple people. These covenants are the basis for all the promises and hopes that are fulfilled in Jesus, the Liberating King. That's why this collection of books, often called the Old Testament, is so important to early Christians. The followers of Jesus found His coming anticipated on almost every page.

So why do we call these books the "Old Testament"? Well, for several reasons. First, there is tradition. For centuries, Christians have referred to these books as the "Old Testament." Bible copyists and publishers used the same terminology for most of church history to designate the first part of the Christian Scriptures. Then, there is Jesus' declaration that He comes to establish a new covenant in His blood. We hear these words first spoken at the last supper when Jesus breaks the bread, blesses God, and invites His followers to "take and eat." That phrase, "new covenant," is identified later with part two of the Christian Bible—the New Testament. If these 27 books from Matthew through Revelation make up the New Testament, then the first part must be, well, the Old Testament.

Seldom, if ever, does anyone stop and ask, "Why?" or, perhaps even more significantly, "What do we mean when we call these books the Old Testament?" Tradition is a powerful factor in how we think. Now I have no real problem with calling these books the Old Testament as long as we do not fill the word "old" with the wrong content. But sometimes we do. If we refer to these books as the Old Testament, with "old" meaning worn out, used up, obsolete, or yesterday's news, then I think we ought to retire the

---

2 Samuel 7:12-16

term altogether. Certainly that's not how Jesus and His followers look at their Bible. For them, it is God's Word. In the Law, Prophets, and Writings of their Bible, the voice of God can be heard and felt. It contains prophecies, stories, and poetry that are ultimately fulfilled in the new covenant inaugurated by the Liberating King. For Jesus and His contemporaries, the "Old Testament" is not "old" at all. It is as fresh as the morning, as relevant as the evening news. They are still waiting for some of its prophecies to be fulfilled. There is no sense that they consider their Scripture old or obsolete. If that is what we mean by "old," we ought to throw a retirement party and be done with it.

But if by "Old" Testament we mean tested, tried, and true,

> if we mean the foundation upon which the New Covenant is built,
>
> if we recognize that these books point toward the climactic moment
> of God's redemption of the world . . .

then why don't we just call it what it is: the First Testament.

As you read, consider the name "First Testament" rather than "Old Testament," and see if it helps you reconsider the value of the Hebrew Scriptures. I suggest that this subtle change might pay big dividends when it comes to thinking about the relationship between part one and part two of the Christian Scriptures. Although this is an oversimplification, the Old Testament stands in relation to the New as promise does to fulfillment, as foundation to temple, as classic to contemporary. You cannot have one without the other. The earlier paves the way and makes the latter possible. That's why the Christian Scriptures contain both Old and New Testaments, or what we prefer to call the First and New Testaments.

As we read through Hebrews, pay attention to how often it appeals to the Hebrew Scriptures. For the writer of this letter, the First Testament is a rich repository of truth and promise that waits for its ultimate fulfillment in the coming of Jesus, God's Son and our Great High Priest. But we must be clear. When Jesus comes to fulfill the promises and covenants, He brings about a better way, a better access to God, a better covenant that is more effective at repairing our broken world. All the earlier promises are concentrated in His work and person, particularly in His work on the cross. The earlier covenants are temporary measures for a chosen people. They are minimally effective in dealing with humanity's true problem. But even this is anticipated in the First Testament when Jeremiah prophesies that God would one day establish a new covenant. The writer of Hebrews picks up on that in chapter 8. He quotes Jeremiah's prophecy at length, reminding his audience that God's chosen people chose to break God's instructions and suffered the consequences. In the new covenant, God promises to write His law on human hearts, establish a permanent relationship with men and women of faith, and erase completely the guilt and consequences of their sins. Unlike the earlier promises, God's work in reconciling the world through the Liberating King is not a temporary measure because Jesus is the final, full, definitive revelation of God.

This letter, written to all Christian believers of Hebrew descent, comes from a leader of their faith residing in Italy who encourages them to stay strong in their new faith. Because of its tone and structure, some have wondered whether this magnificent letter may have been originally a sermon that was later written and circulated as a letter. We can't know for certain. Nor do we need to know. What is certain is that it still speaks to us today.

Chapter 1

FAR ABOVE HEAVENLY MESSENGERS

*S*ince before the first man and woman put their tender feet on earth, God has been at work. But almost immediately, God saw His image in humanity distorted and creation damaged as people disobeyed Him and yearned to be more creator than creature. So God sent prophets, men and women serving as His voice in the world, to call broken people back to the peace and solitude of the garden. But all along, God promised us something more. When the fullness of time arrived, God spoke to us through His Son.

¹Long ago, at different times and in different ways, God's voice came to our ancestors through the *Hebrew* prophets. ²But in these last days, it has come to us through His Son, the One who has been given dominion over all things and through whom all worlds were made.

³This is the One who—imprinted with God's image, shimmering with His glory—sustains all that exists through the power of His word. He was seated at the right hand of the *royal* God once He Himself had made the offering that purified all our sins. ⁴This Son of God is elevated as far above the heavenly messengers as His holy name is elevated above theirs.

*W*hen you think of angels, what comes to mind? Fair, blonde women with downy wings? Floating figures in heavy robes? Most of our ethereal images are influenced by art and pop culture—and are far removed from the Bible. The word "angel" literally means "messenger," and it can refer to either a human being or a heavenly being. The Hebrews author is writing about heavenly messengers.

In the Bible, heavenly messengers have several functions—executors of God's judgment, guardians of God's people, heralds of God's plans. They appear at critical moments to chosen people who play important roles in God's salvation, arriving to announce the birth and resurrection of Jesus and to transmit God's law to Moses. But as important as heavenly messengers have been and continue to be in reconciling humanity to God, to the work of God's own Son as Creator, Sustainer, and Great High Priest, they are no more than messengers. They are created beings who serve the will of God and His Son. Recognizing their place, they bow before the Son in loving adoration.

⁵For no heavenly messengers have ever heard God address them *with these words of the Psalms*:

You are My Son.
    Today I have become Your Father.*

Or *heard Him promise*,

1:5 Psalm 2:7

I will be to You a Father,
    and You will be My Son.*

6Now, when the Son, the firstborn *of God*, was brought into the world, God said,

Let all My heavenly messengers worship Him.*

7Concerning the heavenly messengers, God said,

I make My angels like the winds,
    and My servants like a flame.*

8But to the Son *He said*,

God, Your throne is eternal;
    You will rule Your kingdom with the scepter of justice.
9You have loved what is right
    and hated what is evil;
That is why God, Your God, has anointed You
    with the oil of gladness and lifted You above Your
        companions.*

10And *God continues*,

In the beginning, You, Lord, laid the foundation of the earth
    and set the skies above us with Your own hands.

1:5 2 Samuel 7:14
1:6 Deuteronomy 32:43 (LXX and DSS only)
1:7 Psalm 104:4
1:8-9 Psalm 45:6-7

[11]*But while* they will someday pass away,

> You remain *forever*;
> when they wear out like old clothes,

[12]You will roll them up

> and change them into something new.

But You will never change;

> Your years will never come to an end.*

[13]Did God ever say to any of the heavenly messengers,

Sit here, at My right hand, *in the seat of honor;*

> and I'll put all Your enemies under Your feet?*

[14]*No, of course not.* The heavenly messengers are only spirits and servants, sent out to minister to those who will certainly inherit salvation.

1:10-12 Psalm 102:25-27
1:13 Psalm 110:1

Chapter 2

NOTHING SHORT OF BRILLIANT

*T*he letter to the Hebrew Christians is punctuated with passages that sound an alarm: danger, both imminent and eternal, is at hand. The problem faced by these early believers and by us today is not that we might make a decision to leave the faith for something else. That sometimes happens, but it's rare. The real danger then and now is the gentle erosion of rock-solid commitments. It's not that we go full-speed ahead away from the safety and security of the harbor. It's that we drift, almost imperceptibly, toward the rapids.

The currents that would bring us to peril are often just below the surface. Although they are hidden, they still move rivers, cross oceans, and ultimately shape continents. We may think we have solid foundations, but we should remember how a single drop of water erodes, how a wisp of air grinds down.

How often it happens! A person makes a decision to follow the Liberator. He practically explodes with joy. Then, life happens and the invisible forces that shape culture—in our world, the idols of consumerism, relativism, and materialism—begin their exacting work to shape us into an image that no longer reflects our Savior. Over and over again, the writer warns us to be careful. Don't neglect this great salvation. Make sure the anchor holds.

¹That is why we ought to pay even closer attention to the voice that has been speaking so that we will never drift away from it. ²For if

the words *of instruction and inspiration* brought by heaven's messengers were valid, and *if we live in a universe where* sin and disobedience receive their just rewards, ³then how will we escape *destruction* if we ignore this great salvation? We heard it first from our Lord Jesus, then from those who passed on His teaching. ⁴God also testifies to this truth by signs and wonders and miracles and the gifts of the Holy Spirit lighting on those He chooses.

⁵Now, clearly God didn't set up the heavenly messengers *to bring the final word* or to rule over the world that is coming. ⁶I have read something somewhere:

> I can't help but wonder why You care about mortals
> > or choose to love the son of man.
> ⁷⁻⁸Though born below the heavenly messengers,
> > You honored the son of man like royalty,
> > crowning him with glory and honor,
> Raising him above all earthly things,
> > placing everything under his feet.*

*H*ere is God's Son:
Creator—Sustainer—Great High Priest.
Worshiped by angels.
Seated next to God on His throne.

Someone with these qualifications is perfect for the task of redeeming creation, right? Well, not yet. What made Jesus perfect for the task was something that could only happen on earth. He had to enter our fallen world, take on our feeble flesh, and suffer a violent death at the hands of an angry mob. Suffering is what ultimately made Jesus right for what we needed. What happened next was nothing short of brilliant!

When God placed everything under the Son of Man, He didn't leave out anything. Maybe we don't see all that happening yet; [9]but what we do see is Jesus, born a little lower than the heavenly messengers, who is now crowned with glory and honor because He *willingly* suffered and died. *And He did that* so that through God's grace, He might taste death on behalf of everyone.

[10]It only makes sense that God, by whom and for whom everything exists, would choose to bring many of us to His side by using suffering to perfect Jesus, *the founder of our faith,* the pioneer of our salvation. [11]*As I will show you*, it's important that the One who brings us to God and those who are brought to God become one, *since we are all from one Father*. This is why Jesus was not ashamed to call us His family, [12]saying, *in the words of the psalmist,*

> I will speak Your Name to My brothers and sisters
> > when I praise You in the midst of the community.*

[13]And, *in the words of Isaiah,*

> I will wait for the Eternal One.*

2:12 Psalm 22:22
2:13 Isaiah 8:17

And, again,

> Look, here I am with the children God has given Me.*

[14]Since we, the children, are all creatures of flesh and blood, Jesus took on flesh and blood, so that by dying He could destroy the one who held power over death—the devil—[15]and destroy the fear of death that has always held people captive.

[16]So notice—His concern here is not for the welfare of the heavenly messengers, but for the children of Abraham. [17]He had to become as human as His sisters and brothers *so that when the time came*, He could become a merciful and faithful high priest of God called to reconcile a sinful people. [18]Since He has also been tested by suffering, He can help us when we are tested.

2:13 Isaiah 8:18

*F*or the first-century Jewish-Christian audience, no one plays a more significant role or is more highly revered in the First Testament (Hebrew Scriptures) than Moses. He rescues the mass of Hebrew slaves out of bondage in Egypt. He ascends Mount Sinai to receive God's law and establish a covenant. He shepherds the children of Israel safely through the desert for 40 years and leads them to the brink of the promised land. His faithfulness to God and love for his people is remembered and celebrated in stories and poetry throughout Scripture. He was indeed a remarkable man. Yet Jesus' faithfulness to God and what He accomplished for us is on a totally different level. Moses was indeed faithful to God and accomplished a great deal as God's servant. Jesus, too, was faithful to God, but He accomplished what Moses could not because He's God's very own Son.

¹So, all of you who are holy partners in a heavenly calling, let's turn our attention to Jesus, the Emissary *of God* and High Priest who brought us the faith we profess, ²and compare Him to Moses, *who also brought words from God*. Both of them were faithful to their missions, to the One who called them. ³But we value Jesus more than Moses, in the same way that we value a builder more than the house he builds. ⁴Every house is built by someone, but the builder of all things is God. ⁵Moses *brought healing and redemption to his people* as a

faithful servant in God's house, and he was a witness to the things that would be spoken later. [6]But *Jesus,* the Liberating King, was faithful as a Son of that house. (We become that house, if we're able to hold on to the confident hope we have *in God* until the end.)

[7]Listen now, to the voice of the Holy Spirit. *The psalmist wrote,*

Today, if you listen to His voice,
[8]Don't harden your hearts the way they did
   in the bitter uprising *at Meribah*
[9]Where your ancestors tested Me
   though they had seen My marvelous power.
[10]For the 40 years *they traveled on*
   to the land that I had promised them,
That generation *broke My heart.*
Grieving and angry, I said, "Their hearts are unfaithful;
   they don't know what I want from them."
[11]That is why I swore in anger
   they would never enter *salvation's* rest.*

[12]Brothers and sisters, pay close attention so you won't develop an evil and unbelieving heart that causes you to abandon the living God. [13]Encourage each other every day—for as long as we can still say "today"—so none of you let the deceitfulness of sin harden your hearts. [14]*There's no need for it.* For we have become partners with the Liberating King—if we can just hold on to our confidence, *gained when we became faithful,* until the end.

[15]Look at the lines *from the psalm* again:

3:7-11 Psalm 95:7-11

Today, if you listen to His voice,
Don't harden your hearts the way they did
   in the bitter uprising *at Meribah.*

[16]Now who, *exactly, was God talking to then?*—who heard and rebelled? Wasn't it all of those whom Moses led out of Egypt? [17]And who made God angry for an entire generation? Wasn't it those who sinned *against Him,* those whose bodies are still buried in the wilderness, *the site of that uprising?* [18]It was those disobedient ones who God swore would never enter into salvation's rest. [19]And we can see that they couldn't enter because they did not believe.

¹That's why, as long as that promise of entering God's rest remains open to us, we should be careful that none of us seem to fall short ourselves. ²Those people in the wilderness heard *God's* good news, just as we have heard it, but the message they heard didn't do them any good since it wasn't combined with belief. ³We who believe are entering into salvation's rest, as He said,

> That is why I swore in anger
>> they would never enter *salvation's* rest,*

even though God's works were finished from the very creation of the world. ⁴(For didn't God say that on the seventh day *of creation* He rested from all His works?* ⁵And doesn't God say in the psalm that they would never enter into *salvation's* rest?)*

*T*here is much discussion of "rest" in what we are calling the First Testament. God rests on the seventh day after creation. In the Ten Commandments, God commands His people to remember the Sabbath, to keep it holy. The way to keep it holy, God says, is to do

---

4:3 Psalm 95:11
4:4 Genesis 2:2
4:5 Psalm 95:11

no work that day and rest. The mandate not to work must have sounded strange in the ears of those recently liberated slaves. Only a few months earlier their lives had been all about work. Their aches and pains were a constant reminder of the burden they bore for their Egyptian masters. Now the God who released them commands them to remember the Sabbath day, keep it holy, and do no work. More than any other, the commandment to keep the Sabbath underscores their freedom and celebrates the fact that they now stand in a new covenant with God. But think about what this means. By letting go of daily work, they declared their absolute dependence on God to meet their needs. In our hustle-and-bustle world, we, too, should remember that we do not live by the work of our hands, but by the bread and Word that God supplies.

But as wonderful as this rest is, a greater rest is yet to come. A day is coming when we will rest from all toil, when we will be released from all suffering, and when we will inherit the earth and all its beauty. Jesus the Liberating King embodies this greater rest that still awaits the people of God, a people fashioned through obedience and faith. If some fail to enter that rest, it is not because God has not called. It is because we fail to answer the call.

[6]So *if God prepared a place of rest*, and those who were given the good news didn't enter because they chose disobedience *over faith*, then it remains open for us to enter. [7]Once again, God has fixed a day, and that day is "today," as David said so much later when he wrote *in the psalm* quoted earlier:

Today, if you listen to His voice,
Don't harden your hearts.*

8Now if Joshua had been able to lead those who followed him into God's rest, would God then have spoken this way? 9There still remains a place of rest, a sort of Sabbath, for the people of God 10because those who enter into salvation's rest lay down their labors in the same way that God entered into a Sabbath rest from His.

11So let us move forward to enter this rest, so that none of us fall into the kind of faithless disobedience that prevented them from entering. 12The word of God, *you see*, is alive and moving; sharper than a double-edged sword; piercing the divide between soul and spirit, joints and marrow; able to judge the thoughts and will of the heart. 13No creature can hide from God: God sees all. Everyone and everything is exposed, opened for His inspection, and He's the One we will have to explain ourselves to.

*T*he word of God is powerful. When God uttered the word, the worlds were created. By God's word everything finds a rhythm, a place, an order. God's word fills, empowers, enlivens, and redeems us. But its powers of creation and redemption are only one edge of God's double-edged sword. The word cuts both ways. The same word that creates and redeems also divides and destroys. It pierces and exposes us. It lays us bare.

Thanks be to God.

---

[14]Since we have a great High Priest, Jesus, the Son of God who has passed through the heavens *from death into new life with God,* let us hold tightly to our faith. [15]For Jesus is not some high priest who has no sympathy for our weaknesses *and flaws.* He has already been tested in every way that we are tested; but He emerged victorious, without failing God. [16]So let us step boldly to the throne of grace, where we can find mercy and grace to help when we need it most.

*T*hroughout the Scriptures, priests are key players. They serve as mediators between God and humanity, communicating to us God's grace and carrying our concerns to God.

God → priest → a person   A priest communicates God's love
                           and grace to us

God ← priest ← a person   A priest carries our concerns to
                           God

When Hebrews refers to Jesus as the Great High Priest, it is because He accomplishes something beautiful and unique by becoming the sacrifice that atones for sins once and for all. But the fact that Jesus is our High Priest and the ultimate sacrifice doesn't set aside our need—or God's call—that we be priests for each other. You see, the same Bible that assigns Jesus so lofty a role as Great High Priest, seated with God upon the throne of heaven, also says, "own up to your sins to one another and pray for one another. In the end you may be healed." These are not mutually exclusive ideas.

Martin Luther, one of the early reformers, often wrote about "the priesthood of all believers." He realized that every baptized believer can be—indeed must be—a priest for someone else. You see, Luther lived at a time when priests were a special class of people and there was considerable distance between priests and the people. Some priests, backed by powerful people, abused their priestly duties and took advantage of others. Luther, himself a Catholic monk, had a fresh encounter with God when he read the Scriptures. God was doing something new. He came to believe that as we follow Jesus, the Great High Priest, we must become priests too. Paul said it this way: the same God who pursued us and brought us back into a restored and healthy relationship with Him through the Liberating King has now given us the same calling to pursue others on His behalf to bring them back to their Creator God.*

Here's what I mean: Whenever you share a cup of cold water in Jesus' name, you're a priest. You're communicating the grace of God in the gift of cool, clean water. Whenever you pray for another person, you're a priest. You're carrying the concerns and needs of another to heaven. Whenever you share the good news of God's love with someone, you're working as a priest. You are a conduit for the best news anyone could ever hear.

But if we are honest, there are times that we need a priest too, right? There are problems and pains so deep, sins so intractable, that we need a person of flesh and blood—someone we can touch, hear, and see to hear and help us. God has taken care of that too. That is why God prepared for His Son a body. If we are to be like Him, we must be a priest and allow someone else to be a priest for us. We may not call them "priests" or think of them as priests, but that is what we are doing. When we say, "pray for me," we're saying, "I need a priest." We need someone to join us in carrying our con-

2 Corinthians 5:15-20

cerns to God. When we hear the gospel spoken, preached, pro-
claimed, and receive some blessing, we're receiving God's grace
through the mouth of a priest.

The Great High Priest ever lives to intercede for us. No one of us
here below can match His work. Nor should we try. But He invites us
to follow Him and join in His heavenly work.

[1]*Remember what I said earlier about the role of the high priest,* even the
ones chosen by human beings? The job of every high priest is reconciliation: approaching God on behalf of others and offering Him
gifts and sacrifices to repair the damage caused by our sins *against
God and each other.* [2]The high priest should have compassion for
those who are ignorant of the faith and those who fall out of the
faith because he also has wrestled with human weakness, [3]and so
the priest must offer sacrifices both for his sins and for those of
the people. [4]*The office of high priest and* the honor that goes along
with it isn't one that someone just takes. One must be set aside,
called by God, just as God called Aaron, *the brother of Moses.*

[5]In the same way, the Liberating King didn't call Himself but was
appointed to His priestly office by God, who said to Him,

You are My Son.
Today I have become Your Father,*

[6]and who also says elsewhere,

You are a priest forever—
    in the *honored* order of Melchizedek.*

[7]When Jesus was *on the earth, a creature of* flesh *and blood,* He offered up prayers and pleas, groans and tears to the One who could save Him from death. He was heard because He approached God with reverence. [8]Although He was a Son, Jesus learned obedience through the things He suffered [9]and was perfected *through that suffering* so that He could become the way of eternal salvation for all those who hear and follow Him [10]and could be—as God called Him to be—a High Priest in the order of Melchizedek.

[11]I have a lot more to say about this, but it may be hard for you to follow since you've become dull in your understanding. [12]By this time you ought to be teachers yourselves, yet I feel like you want me to reteach you the most basic things that God wants you to know. It's almost like you're *a baby again, coddled at your mother's breast,* nursing, not ready for solid food. [13]No one who lives on milk alone can know the ins and outs of what it means to be righteous *and pursue justice*; that's because he is only a baby. [14]But solid food is for those who have come of age, for those who have learned through practice to distinguish good from evil.

5:6 Psalm 110:4

Chapter 6

A MORE PERFECT UNDERSTANDING

*W*hen Jesus said that we must become like children to enter the kingdom of God, He didn't mean that we should stay children. It's clear that He wanted us to grow and mature in our faith. Those who don't move beyond the basics—tasting the gifts and powers of the new creation, partaking in the Spirit and the word of God—and then fall away bring shame to the Liberating King and produce nothing but briars and brambles. There is no stagnant life in the Kingdom. Either you grow and produce a blessing or you languish and descend into a curse. Be warned.

¹So let's push on toward a more perfect understanding and move beyond just the basic teachings of the Liberating King. There's no reason to rehash the fundamentals: repenting from *what you loved in* your old dead lives, believing in God *as our Creator and Redeemer,* ²teaching about *the importance of* ceremonial washings, *setting aside those called to service through* the ritual laying on of hands, the coming resurrection of those who have died, and God's final judgment *of all people for all time.* ³No, we will move on toward perfection, if God wills it.

⁴⁻⁶It is impossible to restore the changed heart of the one who has fallen from faith—who has already been enlightened, has tasted the gift of new life from God, has shared in the power of the Holy Spirit, and has known the goodness of God's revelation and the

powers of the coming age. If such a person falls away, it's as though that one were crucifying the Son of God all over again and holding Him up to ridicule. [7]*You see*, God blesses the ground that drinks of the rain and then produces a bountiful crop for those who cultivate it. [8]But land that produces nothing but thorns and brambles? That land is worthless and in danger of being cursed, burned to the bare earth.

[9]But *listen*, my friends—we don't mean to completely discourage you with such talk. We are convinced that you are made for better things, the things of salvation, [10]because God is not unjust *or unfair*. He won't overlook the work you have done or the love you have carried to each other in His name while doing His work, as you are still doing. [11]We want you all to continue working until the end so that you'll realize the certainty that comes with hope [12]and not grow lazy. We want you to walk in the footsteps of the faithful *who came before you*, from whom you can learn to be steadfast in pursuing the promises *of God*.

[13]Remember when God made His promise to Abraham? He had to swear by Himself, there being no one greater: [14]"Surely I will bless you and multiply your descendants."* [15]And after Abraham had endured with patience, he obtained the promise he had hoped for. [16]When swearing an oath to confirm what they are saying, humans swear by someone greater than themselves and so bring their arguments to an end. [17]In the same way, when God wanted to confirm His promise as true and unchangeable, He swore an oath to the heirs of that promise. [18]So God has given us two unchanging things: *His promise and His oath*. These prove that it is impossible for God to lie.

6:14 Genesis 22:17

As a result, we who come to God for refuge might be encouraged to seize that hope that is set before us. [19]That hope is real and true, an anchor to steady our *restless* souls, a hope that leads us back behind the curtain *to where God is (as the high priests did in the days when reconciliation flowed from sacrifices in the temple)* [20]and back into the place where Jesus, who went ahead on our behalf, has entered since He has become a High Priest forever in the order of Melchizedek.

*M*elchizedek is perhaps the most mysterious figure in Scripture. He appears for the first time in Genesis 14:17-20 as Abraham returns from battle against Chedorlaomer and his allies. In a place known as the King's Valley, the king of Sodom and Melchizedek go out to meet the victorious Abraham. Melchizedek, the king of Salem—an early name for the city that would become Jerusalem—and priest of the God Most High, carries bread and wine out to Abraham and his companions. He speaks a blessing upon Abraham and God, who has made this victory possible. Abraham, out of gratitude and perhaps out of custom, gives to Melchizedek 10 percent of what he won from the battle. Afterward, Melchizedek is never seen or heard from again.

The name "Melchizedek" shows up again in Psalm 110, a song of David that is widely used to celebrate the coronation of the Davidic kings in Jerusalem. When God installs His king upon the throne of Jerusalem, He promises to vanquish his enemies and establish him as an eternal priest according to the honored order of Melchizedek. Although this promise could apply to any of David's sons who would one day be king, it was especially appropriate for Jesus, David's Son, the Liberating King. It is not by chance that Psalm 110 became the most quoted psalm in reference to Jesus, celebrating His ascension to God's right hand.

But who was Melchizedek? Who was this enigmatic figure

stepping out of the shadows only to return again where he came? He brought bread and wine to Abraham after the battle was won, the same elements Jesus would break and bless during the last supper, saying, "Take eat, this is My body. . . . Take, drink, this is the blood of the new covenant." Melchizedek, the priest of the Most High, blessed our Father Abraham and received his tithes—the first tithes given in the Scriptures—long before the priesthood was established. So who was Melchizedek really?

These puzzling texts and images fostered a lot of speculation among spiritually minded Jews in Jesus' day. The Jews who left behind the library we know today as the Dead Sea Scrolls wrote several texts about this baffling figure. In one of these ancient scrolls (11QMelchizedek), Melchizedek is more than he seems; he is a heavenly messenger who returns at the end of days to exercise God's final judgment and deliver "the sons of light" from the powers of darkness. While most of these amazing scrolls are fragmentary, it seems these pious Jews identified Melchizedek with the archangel Michael, one of the most important angels in heaven. This perspective on Melchizedek made sense to devout Jews who realized that Melchizedek appears without reference to his parents. In the First Testament, everybody is "the son of" somebody, right? And how could someone serve as a priest of the Most High *forever*? "Maybe Melchizedek is more than a man and serves in some heavenly temple," they concluded.

In this Book of Hebrews, Jesus is often referred to as "a priest forever according to the order of Melchizedek." Psalm 110 was never far away as the writer unpacked this theme. Melchizedek is taken as a type of Jesus, and the few details we know about him are mined and sculpted into a beautiful image of how Jesus' priesthood belongs to an ancient, perhaps heavenly, order of priests that contrasts the temple priests in Jerusalem.

Hundreds of years after Abraham receives Melchizedek's blessing, God establishes an earthly priesthood through Moses and Aaron, a priesthood identified with the sons of Levi. God commands the Levites to collect 10 percent (a tithe) from the children of Abraham to demonstrate their fidelity to God's covenant promises. But these latter-day priests belong to an order that had already paid tithes to Melchizedek. Although it is foreign to those of us born into individualistic, Western societies, ancient people understand that all the children of Abraham—even the Levites—are, in a sense, located in Abraham by virtue of their genealogy. They are "the seed of Abraham," and so they are present in him the day he receives Melchizedek's blessing and pays the tithe of his spoils. By virtue of their ancestry, when Abraham is blessed, all future Levites are blessed through him. When Abraham pays tithes, all future Levites pay tithes. And since the one who blesses is greater than the one blessed and the one who receives tithes is greater than the one who pays them, Melchizedek (and Jesus who shares his status) is ranked higher than those priests who serve in Jerusalem's temple. If any Christians might now be tempted to cover their sins and guilt by appeal to the priests in Jerusalem, they should well remember the reality that Jesus, like Melchizedek before Him, occupies a higher rank. He exercises an eternal priesthood whereby sin and guilt are taken away for good.

Some have wondered whether Melchizedek is actually the Liberating King, a manifestation of God's Son in the early, raw days of God's dealings with Abraham and his people. After all, the name "Melchizedek" means "king of righteousness," and his role as king of Salem makes him the "king of peace (*shalom*)." Both righteousness and peace characterize the gentle rule of the Liberating King and become part of the standard vocabulary of faith. But this letter doesn't demand this association. It demands only that we see what prophets and sages had seen already. This mysterious Melchizedek, king of righteousness and peace, was a precursor to the Prince of Peace. In his brief appearance in Genesis and in Psalms, he opened a window into the mystery of God and His plan to redeem the world. With Melchizedek, we see an eternal priest who represents a higher order of kings and priests that includes Jesus who comes to rule the world with justice and to exercise perfectly an eternal priesthood.

[1] *In the Book of Genesis, we read about* when Melchizedek, the king of Salem and priest of the Most High God, met Abraham as he returned from defeating *King Chedorlaomer* and his allies. Melchizedek blessed our ancestor, and [2] Abraham gave him a tenth of everything captured in the battle.*

Let's look more closely at Melchizedek. First, his name means "king of righteousness"; and *his title*, king of Salem, means "king of peace." [3] The Scriptures don't name his mother or father or descendants, and they don't record his birth or his death. We could say he's like the Son of God: eternal, a priest forever.

[4] And just imagine how great this man was, that even our *great and honorable* patriarch Abraham gave him a tenth of the spoils.

7:2 Genesis 14:17-20

⁵Compare him to the priests *who serve in our temple,* the descendants of Levi, who were given a commandment in the law *of Moses to collect one-tenth of the income of the tribes of Israel.* The priests took that tithe from their own people, even though they were also descended from Abraham. ⁶But this man, *Melchizedek,* who did not belong to that Levite ancestry, collected a tenth part of Abraham's income; and although Abraham had received the promises, it was Melchizedek who blessed Abraham. ⁷Now I don't have to tell you that it is the lesser one who receives a blessing from the greater, *so Melchizedek must be considered superior even to the patriarch from whom we descend.* ⁸*In the case of the priests descended from Levi,* they are mortal men who receive a tithe *of one-tenth;* but the Scriptures record no death of *Melchizedek,* the one who received Abraham's tithe. ⁹I guess you could even say that Levi, who receives our tithes, originally paid tithes through Abraham ¹⁰because he was still unborn and only a part of his ancestor when Abraham met Melchizedek.

¹¹If a perfect method *of reconciling with God*—a perfect priesthood—had been found in the sons of Levi (a priesthood that communicated God's law to the people), then why *would the Scriptures* speak of another priest, a priest according to the order of Melchizedek, instead of, say, from the order of Aaron? What would be the need for it? *It would reflect a new way of relating to God* ¹²because when there is a change in the priesthood there must be a corresponding change in the law as well. ¹³We're talking about someone who comes from another tribe, from which no member has ever served at God's altar. ¹⁴It's clear that *Jesus,* our Lord, descended from the tribe of Judah, but Moses never spoke about priests from that tribe. ¹⁵Doesn't it seem obvious? *Jesus is* a priest who resembles Melchizedek *in so many ways;* ¹⁶He is someone who

has become a priest not because of some requirement about human lineage but because of the power of a life without end. [17]*Remember, the psalmist* says,

> You are a priest forever—
>> in the *honored* order of Melchizedek.*

[18]Because the earlier commandment was weak and did not reconcile us to God effectively, it was set aside—[19]after all, the law could not make anyone or anything perfect. God has now introduced a new and better hope, through which we may draw near to Him, [20]and confirmed it by swearing to it. [21]The *Levite order of* priests took office without an oath, but this man *Jesus* became a priest through God's oath:

> The Eternal One has sworn an oath
>> and cannot change His mind:
> You are a priest forever.*

[22]So we can see that Jesus has become the guarantee of a *new and better* covenant. [23]Further, the prior priesthood *of the sons of Levi* has included many priests because death cut short their service, [24]but Jesus holds His priesthood permanently because He lives His resurrected life forever. [25]From such a vantage He is able to save those who approach God through Him for all time because He will forever live to be their advocate *in the presence of God.*

[26]It is only fitting that we should have a High Priest who is

---

7:17 Psalm 110:4
7:21 Psalm 110:4

devoted to God, blameless, pure, *compassionate toward but* separate from sinners, and exalted by God to the highest place of honor. [27]Unlike other high priests, He does not first need to make atonement every day for His own sins, and only then for His people's, because He already made atonement, reconciling us with God once and forever when He offered Himself as a sacrifice. [28]The law made imperfect men high priests; but after that law was given, God swore an oath that made His perfected Son a high priest for all time.

Chapter 8

A NEW COVENANT

*W*hen God gave the law to Moses and Israel at Mount Sinai, He appointed a tribe to serve as priests among the people. He set up a system of repentance, restitution, and sacrifices that would help to deal with the guilt and some of the negative consequences of sin. But neither the law nor the actions of Israel's priests could deal effectively with the harm sin continued to do to His creation. Sin had to be dealt a lethal blow, and no one from our world of copies and shadows could eradicate it. Salvation would come, God had promised, but it must come from above where realities and patterns reside.

¹So let me sum up what we've covered so far, *for there is much we have said*: we have a High Priest, *a perfect Priest* who sits *in the place of honor* in the highest heavens, at the right hand of the throne of the Majestic One, ²a Minister within the *heavenly* sanctuary set up by the Lord, not by human hands.

³*As I have said*, it is the role of every high priest to offer gifts and sacrifices *to God,* so clearly this Priest of ours must have something to offer as well. ⁴If He were on earth, then He would not be a priest at all because there are already priests who can offer gifts according to the law *of Moses, and they offer worship daily in a sanctuary set up according to the laws of God given to Moses*—⁵a sanctuary that is only a copy and shadow of the heavenly sanctuary. *We know this, because* God

admonished Moses as he set up the tent for the Lord's sanctuary: "Be sure that you make everything according to the pattern I showed you on the mountain."* [6]But now Jesus has taken on a new and improved priestly ministry; and in that respect, He has been made the Mediator of a better covenant established on better promises. [7]Remember, if the first covenant had been able to reconcile everyone to God, there would be no reason for a second covenant.

*J*eremiah was known as the prophet of the new covenant. Hundreds of years before the birth of the Liberating King, Jeremiah heard the voice of God and saw what God had planned: a new day. A new law inscribed in the mind, written on the heart. A new and abiding knowledge of God. A new covenant where mercy runs deep and sins are forgiven and forgotten.

[8]God found fault with the priests when He said *through the prophet Jeremiah*:

"Look! The time is coming," the Eternal Lord says,
    "when I will bring about a new covenant with the people of
        Israel and Judah.
[9]It will not be like the covenant I made with their ancestors
    when I took them by the hand
    and led them out of *slavery in* the land of Egypt.
They did not remain faithful to that covenant,

---

so," the Eternal One says, "I turned away from them.

[10]But when those days are over," the Eternal One says, "I will make
this *kind of* covenant with the people of Israel:

I will put My laws on their minds

and write them upon their hearts.

I will be their God,

and they will be My people.

[11]*In those days*, they won't need to teach each other *My ways*

or to say to each other, 'Know the Eternal.'

In those days, all will know Me,

from the least to the greatest.

[12]I will be merciful when they fail,

and I will erase their sins *and wicked acts* out of My memory

as though they had never existed."*

[13]With the words "a new covenant," God made the first covenant old;
and what is old and no longer effective will soon fade away completely.

8:8-12 Jeremiah 31:31-34

Chapter 9

A MORE PERFECT SANCTUARY

¹*Think about that first covenant for a moment.* Even that covenant had *rules and* regulations about how to worship and *how to set up* an earthly sanctuary *for God.* ²*In the Book of Exodus,* * *we read how* the first tent was set aside for worship—we call it the holy place—how inside it they placed an oil lamp, a table, and the bread that was consecrated *to God.* ³Behind a second *dividing* curtain, there was another tent which is called the most holy of holy places. ⁴In there, they placed the golden incense altar and the golden ark of the covenant. Inside the ark were the golden urn that contained manna *(the miraculous food God gave our ancestors in the desert),* Aaron's rod that budded,* and the tablets of the covenant *that Moses brought down from the mountain.* ⁵Above the ark were the *golden images of* heavenly beings* of glory who shadowed the mercy seat.

I cannot go into any greater detail about this now; *I don't have the time and space.* ⁶*Here's my point:* When all is prepared as it is supposed to be, the priests go back and forth daily into the first tent to carry out the duties described in the law. ⁷But once a year, the high priest goes alone into that second tent, the holy of holies, with blood to offer for himself and the unwitting errors of the people. ⁸As long as that first tent is standing, the Holy Spirit shows us, the way into the most holy of holy places has not yet been revealed

---

9:2 Exodus 25–26
9:4 Numbers 17:1-13
9:5 Greek *cheroubin*, a class of angels

to us. [9]That first tent symbolizes the present time, when gifts and sacrifices can be offered; but it can't change the *heart and* conscience of the worshiper. [10]These gifts and sacrifices deal only with regulations for the body—food and drink and various kinds of *ritual* cleansings necessary until the time comes to make things truly right.

[11]When the Liberating King arrived as High Priest of the good that comes to us, *He entered* through a greater and more perfect sanctuary that was not part of the earthly creation or made by human hands. [12]He entered once for all time into the most holy of holy places, entering not with the blood of goats or calves *or some other prescribed animal*, but offering His own blood and thus obtaining redemption for us for all time. [13]*Think about it:* if the blood of bulls or of goats, or the sprinkling of ashes from a heifer, restores the defiled to bodily cleanliness *and wholeness*, [14]then how much more powerful is the blood of the Liberating King, who through the eternal Spirit offered Himself as a spotless *sacrifice* to God, purifying your conscience from the dead things *of the world* to the service of the living God?

[15]This is why Jesus is the Mediator of the new covenant: through His death, He delivered us from the sins that we had built up under the first covenant, and His death has made it possible for all who are called to receive God's promised inheritance. [16]For whenever there is a testament—a will—the death of the one who made it must be confirmed [17]because a will takes effect only at the death of its maker; it has no validity as long as the maker is still alive. [18]Even the first *testament—the first covenant*—required blood to be put into action. [19]When Moses had given all the laws of God to the people, he took the blood of calves and of goats, water,

hyssop, and scarlet wool, and he sprinkled the scroll and all the people, [20]telling them, "This is the blood of the covenant that God has commanded for us."* [21]In the same way, he also sprinkled blood upon the sanctuary and upon the vessels used in worship. [22]Under the law, it's almost the case that everything is purified in connection with blood; without the shedding of blood, sin cannot be forgiven.

*H*ere we are reminded that what is most real, what is most true, is the unseen reality. What appears real to the naked eye is, in fact, flimsy and temporary, lacking true substance. Take the temple in Jerusalem, the holiest place on earth. It seemed real enough, with its massive stone construction, constant flurry of rituals, and daily offerings. But the writer tells us that as real as it appeared, it was merely a copy or shadow of another place, the heavenly temple. Whatever took place in this shadowy temple down below may have provided some temporary relief from the ills that plagued God's people, but it could not change the realities of alienation from God, sin, and death.

Every year on a most special day, the Day of Atonement, the high priest would don his priestly garb and enter the most holy of holy places in the temple. His task was profound, his duty dangerous: he must appear before God carrying the sins of his people. All the sins of Israel were concentrated in him as he carried the blood of the sacrifice into the divine presence. Imagine this man embodying the sins of a nation and appearing before pure Holiness. How could such a man stand? Despite the drama enacted every year in Jerusalem on the Day of Atonement, sin and death never let up on its assault.

But there was another day, a Day of Atonement unlike any other, when Jesus the Liberating King concentrated in Himself the sins of the world, hanging on a cross not far from the temple's holiest chamber. Indeed, for a time, He became sin.* But unlike the high priest in the earthly copy of the temple, the writer tells us that, crucified and raised, He entered the true temple of heaven and was ushered into the divine presence. He who had embodied the sins of the world carried His own blood into the holy presence. At that moment, everything changed.

[23]*Since what was given in the old covenant was* the earthly sketch of the heavenly reality, this was sufficient to cleanse the earthly sanctuary; but in heaven, a more perfect sacrifice was needed. [24]The Liberating King did not enter into handcrafted sacred spaces, imperfect copies of heavenly originals, but into heaven itself, where He stands in the presence of God on our behalf. [25]There He does not offer Himself over and over as a sacrifice (as the high priest on earth does when he enters the most holy of holy places each year with blood other than his own) [26]because that would require His repeated suffering since the beginning of the world. No, He has appeared once now, at the end of the age, to put away sin forever by offering Himself as a sacrifice.

---

2 Corinthians 5:16

[27]Just as mortals are appointed to die once and then to experience a judgment, [28]so the Liberating King was offered once *in death* to bear the sins of many and will appear a second time, not to deal again with sin, but to rescue those who eagerly await His return.

Chapter 10

ONCE AND FOR ALL TIME

¹We have seen how the law is simply a shadow of the good things to come. Since it is not the perfect form of these ultimate realities, the offering year after year of these imperfect sacrifices cannot bring perfection to those who come forward to worship. ²If they had served this purpose, wouldn't the repetition of these sacrifices have become unnecessary? If they had worked—and cleansed the worshipers—then one sacrifice would have taken away their consciousness of sin. ³But these sacrifices actually remind us that we sin *again and again*, year after year. ⁴In the end, the blood of bulls and of goats is powerless to take away sins. ⁵So when Jesus came into the world, He said,

> Sacrifices and offerings were not what You wanted,
> but instead a body that You prepared for Me.
> ⁶Burnt offerings and sin offerings
> were not what pleased You.
> ⁷Then I said, "See, I have come to do Your will, God,
> as it is inscribed of Me in the scroll of the book."*

⁸Now when it says that God doesn't want and He takes no real pleasure in sacrifices, burnt offerings, and sin offerings (even though the law calls for them), ⁹and follows this with "See, I have come to do Your will,"* He effectively takes away the first—*animal*

10:5-7 Psalm 40:6-8
10:9 Psalm 40:7

sacrifice—in order to establish the second, *more perfect sacrifice.* ¹⁰By God's will, we are made holy through the offering of the body of Jesus the Liberating King, once and for all time.

¹¹*In the first covenant,* every day every priest stands at his post serving, offering over and over those same sacrifices that can never take away sin. ¹²But when the Liberator stepped up to offer His single sacrifice for sins for all time, He sat down *in the position of honor* at the right hand of God. ¹³Since then, He has been waiting for the day when He rests His feet on His enemies' backs,* *as the psalm says.* ¹⁴With one *perfect* offering, Jesus has perfected forever those who are being made holy, ¹⁵as the Holy Spirit keeps testifying to us *through the prophet Jeremiah.* After he says:

¹⁶"But when those days are over," says the Eternal One, "I will make
  this *kind of* covenant with the people *of Israel*:
I will put My laws in their hearts
  and write them upon their minds."*

Then He adds,

¹⁷I will erase their sins and wicked acts out of My memory
  *as though they had never existed.**

¹⁸When there is forgiveness such as this, there is no longer any need to make an offering for sin.

¹⁹So, my friends, Jesus by His blood gives us courage to enter the

---

10:13 Psalm 110:1
10:16 Jeremiah 31:33
10:17 Jeremiah 31:34

most holy of holy places. [20]He has created for us a new and living way through the curtain *to the holy place*, that is, through His flesh. [21]Since we have a great High Priest who presides over the house of God, [22]let us draw near with true hearts full of faith, with hearts rinsed clean of any evil conscience, and with bodies cleansed with pure water.

*T*he Christian faith is a communal faith: it is birthed in the community of persons we call the Trinity, and it is lived out most fearlessly in the church. The word translated "church" in English Bibles means literally "assembly of the called"; it implies that we have said "yes" to God's call in our lives. We assemble because we are "the called," called into being by God Himself. The same voice that said, "Let there be light" in the beginning continues to call us, "Let there be the church." Some people, for reasons only they know, choose to live their Christian faith in isolation. When they do, they cut themselves off from the gifts, encouragement, and vitality of others. And perhaps, just as tragically, they deprive the church of the grace and life God has invested in them.

[23]Let us hold strong to the confession of our hope, never wavering, since the One who promised it to us is faithful. [24]Let us consider how to inspire each other to greater love and to righteous deeds, [25]not forgetting to gather as a community, as some have forgotten, but encouraging each other, especially as the day *of His return* approaches.

[26]Now if we willfully persist in sin after receiving such knowledge of the truth, then there is no sacrifice left for those sins,

[27]only the fearful prospect of judgment and a fierce fire that will consume God's adversaries. [28]*Remember that* those who depart from the law of Moses are put to death without mercy based on the testimony of two or three witnesses.* [29]Just think how much more severe the punishment will be for those who have turned their backs on the Son of God, trampled on the blood of the covenant by which He made them holy, and outraged the Spirit of grace *with their contempt.* [30]For we know the God who said, "Vengeance belongs to Me— I will repay,"* also said, "The Eternal One will judge His people."* [31]It is truly a frightening thing to be on the wrong side of the living God.

[32]Instead, think back to the days after you first became enlightened *and understood who Jesus was:* when you endured all sorts of suffering *in the name of the Lord*, [33]when people held you up for public scorn and ridicule, or when they abused your partners and companions in the faith. [34]Remember how you had compassion for those in prison and how you cheerfully accepted the seizure of your possessions, knowing that you have a far greater and more enduring possession. [35]Remember this, and do not abandon your confidence, which will lead to rich rewards. [36]Simply endure, for when you have done as God requires of you, you will receive the promise. [37]*As the prophet Habakkuk said,*

> In a little while, *only a little longer,*
>   the One who is coming will come without delay.
> [38]But My righteous one must live by faith,

10:28 Deuteronomy 17:6
10:30 Deuteronomy 32:35
10:30 Deuteronomy 32:36

for if he gives up his commitment,
My soul will have no pleasure in him.*

[39]*My friends*, we are not those who give up hope and so are lost; but we are of the company who live by faith and so are saved.

Chapter 11

COMMENDED BY GOD

*S*tories of faith and faithfulness make up most of the First Testament. The writer of Hebrews recalls some of the most memorable examples of how people of faith lived their lives. But what is faith? Faith is more than belief; it is trust, assurance, and firm conviction. Faith seeks understanding and makes understanding possible. And ultimately, faith is what commends us to God. Ironically, most of those who lived by faith never fully realized the promises God had made. Like us, they journeyed as strangers and exiles, longing for another country. We should remember their patient faith when we face prolonged hardships and allow the trials to strengthen our faith rather than destroy it.

¹Faith is the assurance of things you have hoped for, the absolute conviction that there are realities you've never seen. ²It was by faith that our forebears were approved. ³Through faith, we understand that the universe was created by the word of God; everything we now see was fashioned from that which is invisible.

⁴By faith, Abel presented to God a sacrifice more acceptable than *his brother* Cain's. *By faith,* Abel learned he was righteous, as God Himself testified by approving his offering. And by faith, he still speaks, although his voice was silenced by death.

⁵By faith, Enoch was carried up *into heaven* so that he did not see death; no one could find him because God had taken him. Before he

was taken up, it was said of him that he had pleased God. [6]Without faith, no one can please God because the one coming to God must believe He exists, and He rewards those who come seeking.

[7]By faith, Noah respected God's warning regarding *the flood—the likes of* which no one had ever seen—and built an ark that saved his family. In this, he condemned the world and inherited the righteousness that comes by faith.

[8]By faith, Abraham heard God's call to travel to a place he would one day receive as an inheritance; and he obeyed, not knowing where God's call would take him. [9]By faith, he journeyed to the land of the promise as a foreigner; he lived in tents, as did Isaac and Jacob, his fellow heirs to the promise, [10]because Abraham looked ahead to a city with foundations, a city laid out and built by God.

[11]By faith, *Abraham's wife* Sarah became fertile long after menopause because she believed God would be faithful to His promise. [12]So from this man, who was almost at death's door, God brought forth descendants, as many as the stars in the sky and as impossible to count as the sands of the shore.

[13]All these I have mentioned died in faith without receiving the full promises, although they saw the fulfillment as though from a distance. These people accepted and confessed that they were strangers and foreigners on this earth [14]because people who speak like this make it plain that they are still seeking a homeland. [15]If this was only a bit of nostalgia for a time and place they left behind, then certainly they might have turned around and returned. [16]But such saints as these look forward to a far better place, a heavenly country. So God is not ashamed to be called their God because He has prepared a *heavenly* city for them.

[17]By faith, Abraham, when he endured God's testing, offered *his*

beloved son Isaac *as a sacrifice.* The one who had received God's promise was willing to offer his only son; [18]God had told him, "It is through Isaac that your descendants will bear your name,"* [19]and he concluded that God was capable of raising him from the dead, which, figuratively, is indeed what happened.

[20]By faith, Isaac spoke blessings upon his sons, Jacob and Esau, concerning things yet to come.

[21]By faith, Jacob, when he was dying, blessed the sons of *his son* Joseph, bowing in worship as he leaned upon his staff.*

[22]By faith, Joseph, at his life's end, predicted that the children of Israel would make an exodus from Egypt; and he gave instructions that his bones *be buried in the land they would someday reach.*

[23]By faith, Moses' parents hid him for three months after he was born because they saw that he was handsome; and they did not fear Pharaoh's directive *that all male Hebrew children were to be slain.*

[24]By faith, Moses, when he was grown, refused to be identified solely as the son of Pharaoh's daughter [25]and chose instead to share the sufferings of the people of God, not just living in sin and ease for a time. [26]He considered the abuse *that he and the people of God had* suffered in anticipation of the Liberator more valuable than all the riches of Egypt because he looked ahead to the coming reward.

[27]By faith, Moses left Egypt, unafraid of Pharaoh's wrath and moving forward as though he could see the invisible God. [28]Through faith, he instituted the Passover and the sprinkling of blood *on the doorposts among the Hebrews* so that the destroyer of the firstborn would pass over their homes without harming them. [29]By faith, the

---

11:18 Genesis 21:12
11:21 Genesis 47:31

people crossed through the Red Sea as if they were walking on dry land, although the pursuing Egyptian *soldiers* were drowned when they tried to follow.

³⁰By faith, the walls of Jericho toppled after the people had circled them for seven days. ³¹By faith, the prostitute Rahab welcomed the *Hebrew* spies *into her home* so that she did not perish with the unbelievers.

³²I could speak more *of faith*; I could talk until time itself ran out. If I continued, I could speak *of the examples* of Gideon, Barak, Samson, and Jephthah, of David and Samuel and all the prophets. ³³*I could give accounts of* people alive with faith who conquered kingdoms, brought justice, obtained promises, and closed the mouths of hungry lions. ³⁴*I could tell you how people of faith* doused raging fires, escaped the edge of the sword, made the weak strong, and, stoking great valor among the champions of God, sent opposing armies into panicked flight.

³⁵I could speak of faith bringing women their loved ones back from death and how the faithful accepted torture instead of earthly deliverance because they believed they would obtain a better *life in the* resurrection. ³⁶Others suffered mockery and whippings; they were placed in chains and in prisons. ³⁷The faithful were stoned, sawn in two,* killed by the sword, clothed only in sheepskins and goatskins; they were penniless, afflicted, and tormented. ³⁸The world was not worthy of these saints. They wandered across deserts, crossed mountains, and lived in the caves, cracks, and crevasses of the earth.

³⁹These, though commended by God for their great faith,

11:37 Some early manuscripts read "sawn in two." Other early manuscripts read "tempted." Later manuscripts have both.

did not receive what was promised. [40]That promise has awaited us, who receive the better thing that God has provided *in these last days*, so that with us, our forebears might finally see the promise completed.

*W*e are not alone. We may feel like we are the only ones, but we aren't. We are surrounded by a cloud of martyrs, an army of witnesses. They have run the race of faith and finished well. They have passed the baton to us. It is now our turn. They are pulling for us, praying for us, cheering us on. But how will we run? Will we run our own race or try to run somebody else's? Will our pace be slackened by the weight of guilt and sin? Will we grow tired and give up before the end? Before we know it, we'll pass the baton of faith and take our place in the stands with the witnesses.

¹So since we stand surrounded by *all those who have gone before,* an enormous cloud of witnesses, let us drop every extra weight, every sin that clings to us *and slackens our pace,* and let us run with endurance the long race set before us. ²Now stay focused on Jesus, who designed and perfected our faith. He endured the cross and ignored the shame *of that death* because He focused on the joy that was set before Him; and now He is seated beside God on the throne, *a place of honor.*

³Consider *the life of* the One who endured such *personal attacks and* hostility from sinners so that you will not grow weary or lose heart. ⁴Among you, in your striving against sin, none has resisted *the pressure* to the point of death, as He did.

*G*od *disciplines* His *disciples*. The words look so similar because at the heart of both is "training." Life—with all its hardships and hostilities—is God's training ground for those who belong to Him. What is He training us for? Ironically, He's training us for life—to live and to live well. Not just to live here and now, but to have life in the age to come. He's training us to share His life and holiness. He's training us so that we might finish the race of faith with strength and endurance. He's training us so that our lives might be instruments of peace and justice.

⁵Indeed, you seem to have forgotten the proverb directed to you as children:

> My child, do not ignore the instruction that comes from the
>   Lord,
>   or lose heart when He steps in to correct you;
> ⁶For the Lord disciplines those He loves,
>   and He corrects each one He takes as His own.*

⁷Endure hardship as God's discipline *and rejoice* that He is treating you as His children, for what child doesn't experience discipline from a parent? ⁸But if you are not experiencing the correction that all true children receive, then it may be that you are not His children after all. ⁹Remember, when our human parents disciplined us, we respected them. *If that was true,* shouldn't we respect and live un-

---

12:5-6 Proverbs 3:11-12

der the correction of the Father of all spirits even more? ¹⁰Our parents corrected us for a time as seemed good to them, but God only corrects us to our good so that we may share in His holiness.

¹¹*I'll admit it:* when punishment is happening, it never seems pleasant, only painful. Later, though, it yields the peaceful fruit called righteousness to everyone who has been trained by it. ¹²So lift up your hands that are dangling and brace your weakened knees. ¹³Make straight paths for your feet so that what is lame *in you* won't be put out of joint, but will heal.

¹⁴Pursue peace with everyone, and holiness, since no one will see God without it. ¹⁵Watch carefully that no one falls short of God's favor, that no well of bitterness springs up to trouble you and throw many others off the path. ¹⁶Watch that no one becomes wicked and vile like Esau, *the son of Isaac,* who for a single meal sold his invaluable birthright. ¹⁷You know *from the stories of the patriarchs* that later, when he wished to claim his blessing, he was turned away. He could not reverse his action even though he shed bitter tears over it.

*T*he Bible is a brutally honest book. It contains stories of liars, murderers, and adulterers; and these are the good guys. If we read the Bible looking only for positive role models, we'll be quickly disappointed. But if we are honest with ourselves and confess our own faults, we will find in Scripture, particularly in the First Testament, that we have much in common with many broken saints of the past. But we must not stay broken. We must follow their path to transformation through repentance and faith. Repentance means a change of heart, a change of mind, and ultimately a change of how we live.

Repentance is not something we can accomplish on our own. God's grace comes to us and enables us to turn away from our sin and to turn back to Him. Some, like Esau, never find their way back. He stands as a perpetual warning to those who refuse to turn back to God. Remember the warning of Jesus: "if you do not consider God's ways and truly change, then friends, you should prepare to face His judgment and eternal death."*

18You have not come to the place that can be touched *(as Israel did at Mount Sinai), to a mountain crowned* with blazing fire, darkness, gloom, and a windstorm, 19or to the blast of a trumpet and the sound of a voice—a voice and message so harsh that the people begged not to hear another word. 20(They could not bear the command that was given: that if even a beast touches the mountain, it must be stoned. 21The sight was so terrible that even Moses said, "I am trembling with fear."*)

22No, instead you have come to Mount Zion, to the city of the living God, to the heavenly Jerusalem, to heavenly messengers unnumbered, *to a joyful feast,* 23to the assembly of the firstborn registered as heaven's citizens, to God the righteous Judge of all, and to the spirits of all the righteous who have been perfected. 24You have come to Jesus, the Mediator of a new covenant *between God and humanity,* and to His sprinkled blood, which speaks a greater word than the blood of Abel *crying out from the earth.*

25See that you don't turn away from the One who is speaking; for

Luke 13:3
12:20-21 Exodus 19:12-13; Deuteronomy 9:19

if the ones who heard and refused the One who spoke on earth faced punishment, then how much more will we suffer if we turn away from the One speaking from heaven—[26]the One whose voice in earlier times shook the earth now makes another promise: "Yet once more I will shake not only the earth, but also the heavens"?* [27]The phrase, "Yet once more," means that those things that can be shaken will be removed and taken away, namely, the *first* creation. As a result, what remains will be those things that cannot be shaken. [28]Therefore, let us all be thankful that we are a part of an unshakeable Kingdom and offer to God worship that pleases Him and reflects the awe and reverence we have toward Him [29]for He is like a fierce fire that consumes everything.*

12:26 Haggai 2:6, 21
12:29 Deuteronomy 4:24

*F*or those attuned to popular culture and political discourse today, there is a lot of talk about values and character. The media doesn't have to probe long before it uncovers examples of immorality and hypocrisy in high places. But values and character are not formed in a vacuum; they are forged in a community of like-minded people. That's why it is important to choose your community carefully; you will adopt the values and character of its people. Hebrews comes to a close by creating a fresh vision of how Christian faith is lived out every day. It calls us to a higher ethic, to these essential qualities of a community formed around the cross:

Love—Hospitality—Identifying with the poor and imprisoned—Fidelity in marriage—Contentment—Loyalty to leaders—Imitation of leaders' faith—Avoidance of strange teaching—Continual praise.

¹Let love continue among you. *Let it be the air you take in, that uncurls within you, and that extends between you.* ²Don't forget to extend your hospitality to all, even to strangers; for *as you know,* some have unknowingly shown kindness to heavenly messengers in this way. ³Remember those imprisoned *for their beliefs* as if you were their cellmate; and care for any who suffer harsh treatment, as you are all one body.

⁴Hold marriage in high esteem, all of you, and keep the marriage bed pure because God will judge those who commit sexual sins.

⁵Keep your lives free from the love of money, and be content with what you have because He has said, "I will never leave you; I will always be by your side."* ⁶Because of this promise, we may boldly say,

> The Lord is my help—
>   I won't be afraid of anything.
> How can anyone harm me?*

⁷Listen to your leaders, who have spoken God's word to you. Notice the fruits of their lives and mirror their faith.

⁸Jesus the Liberating King is always the same: yesterday, today, and forever. ⁹Do not be carried away by diverse and strange ways of believing or worshiping. It is good for the heart to be strengthened by grace, not by *regulations about* what you can eat (which do no good even for those who observe them). ¹⁰We approach an altar from which those who stand before the altar in the tent have no right to eat. ¹¹*In the past,* the bodies of those animals whose blood was carried into the sanctuary by the high priest to take away sin were all burned outside the camp. ¹²(In the same way, Jesus suffered and bled outside the city walls *of Jerusalem* to sanctify the people.)

*I*f we are honest, we have to admit that coming to Christ and entering into His church ruins us—at least as far as this world is concerned. If we identify with Him in His suffering and rejection, we will become a reproachful irritation to the powers that rule this culture. If we ever felt at home in this world, if we ever sensed that we belonged, then we would wake up one day to discover that we will never be at home again until we enter the city of God. By entering into Jesus, our Liberating King, we become citizens of another city, subjects of another king. As long as we are here, we should live as resident aliens longing to go home.

¹³Let's then go out to Him and resolve to bear the insult and abuse that He endured. ¹⁴For as long as we are here, we do not live in any permanent city, but are looking for the city that is to come.

¹⁵Through Jesus, then, let us keep offering to God our own sacrifice, the praise of lips that confess His name without ceasing. ¹⁶Let's not neglect what is good and share what we have, for these sacrifices also please God.

¹⁷Listen to your leaders and submit to their authority *over the community,* for they are on constant watch to protect your souls and someday they must give account. Give them reason to be joyful and not to regret their duty, for that will be of no good to you.

¹⁸⁻¹⁹Pray for us, for we have no doubt that our consciences are clean and that we seek to live honestly in all things. ⁹But please pray for me that I may be restored to you even more quickly.

²⁰Now may the God of peace, who brought the great Shepherd of the sheep, our Lord Jesus, back from the dead through the blood of the new everlasting covenant, ²¹perfect you in every good work as you work God's will. May God do in you *only* those things that are pleasing in His sight, through Jesus the Liberating King, to whom we give glory always and forever. Amen.

²²Please, brothers and sisters, pay attention to this word of exhortation, for I have written only a few words to you.

²³I want to tell you that our brother Timothy has been set free; and if he arrives soon, he will come with me when I see you next.

²⁴Give my greetings to your leaders and to all of God's people. Those of Italy greet you.

²⁵May grace always be with you.

As with many New Testament letters, Hebrews ends with a benediction. A benediction is a transformative word that invites the God who desires to change everything to enter our lives and renovate our world. If we will hear the word and step aside, the God of peace will enter our unrest and the God of grace will be with us. What else do we need?

Nothing.

Section Two // **Appendices**

Index to First Testament Scriptures

The Greatness of the Liberating King*

Jesus Is Greater Than the Prophets 1:1-3 Seven character affirmations:	Jesus Is Greater Than the Angels 1:4-14 Seven Scripture quotations:
Has dominion over all things (v. 2) Creator (v. 2) Shimmering with God's glory (v. 3) Imprinted with God's image (v. 3) Sustainer of all things (v. 3) Savior (v. 3) Exalted Lord (v. 3)	Psalm 2:7 (v. 5) 2 Samuel 7:14 (v. 3) Deuteronomy 32:43 or Psalm 97:7 (v. 6) Psalm 104:4 (v. 7) Psalm 45:6-7 (vv. 8-9) Psalm 102:25-27 (vv. 10-12) Psalm 110:1 (v. 13)

* Chart adapted from *Nelson's Complete Book of Bible Maps & Charts: Old and New Testaments.* © 1993, 1996 Thomas Nelson, Inc., Nashville, Tennessee. All rights reserved. Used by permission.

Jesus as High Priest and the Levitical Priesthood

The difference between the Jesus as High Priest and the Levitical priesthood can be set out this way:

Levitical Priests	Jesus
From the sons of Levi (7:11)	From the tribe of Judah (7:13-14)
The Order of Aaron (7:11)	The Order of Melchizedek (7:15)
Became a priest by physical descent (7:16)	Became a priest by the resurrection (7:16)
Law made nothing perfect (7:18-19)	Better hope (7:19) Better covenant (7:22)
Made priests without an oath (7:20-21)	Made a priest with an oath (7:20-21)
Many priests, death cut short their service (7:23)	Unique Son, permanently held priesthood forever lives to be our advocate (7:25)
Daily atonement for their own sins and then for others' sins (7:27)	Once and forever sacrifice of Himself for others (7:26-27)

Two Covenants Compared*

THE FIRST COVENANT (Hebrews 9:1-10)	THE NEW COVENANT (Hebrews 9:11-28)
Old now that the Liberating King has come (Hebrews 8:13).	A new and better hope brought about by the Liberating King (Hebrews 7:19; 8:6-7).
Originated at Mount Sinai (Galatians 4:24-25).	Originated from the Jerusalem above (Galatians 4:26-27).
Brought death and condemnation (2 Corinthians 3:7-9).	Brings life (Ephesians 2:1-13).
Impossible to obey perfectly because of human weakness and sin (Romans 8:3).	Fulfilled perfectly by Jesus (Luke 22:20; 1 Corinthians 11:25).
Required annual offering for sins (Hebrews 9:7-8; 10:1-4).	Removes sin once for all time and rinses the heart clean (Hebrews 9:12; 10:2, 22).
Restricted access to God (Hebrews 9:7-8).	Opened access to God for all (Hebrews 9:15-16).

* Chart adapted from *Nelson's Complete Book of Bible Maps & Charts: Old and New Testaments.* © 1993, 1996 Thomas Nelson, Inc., Nashville, Tennessee. All rights reserved. Used by permission.

The Plan of the Tabernacle*

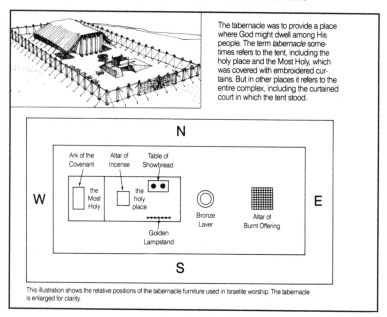

The tabernacle was to provide a place where God might dwell among His people. The term *tabernacle* sometimes refers to the tent, including the holy place and the Most Holy, which was covered with embroidered curtains. But in other places it refers to the entire complex, including the curtained court in which the tent stood.

This illustration shows the relative positions of the tabernacle furniture used in Israelite worship. The tabernacle is enlarged for clarity.

The Plan of Herod's Temple*

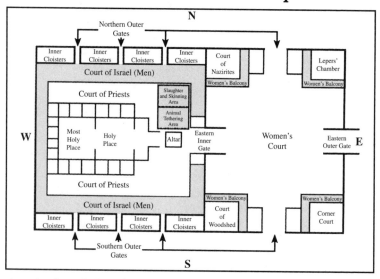

The Works of Faith*

The faith that the readers must maintain is defined in Hebrews 11:1-3 and illustrated in 11:4-40. The triumphs and accomplishments of faith in the lives of Old Testament believers should encourage Christians to "focus on Jesus, who designed and perfected our faith" (12:2).

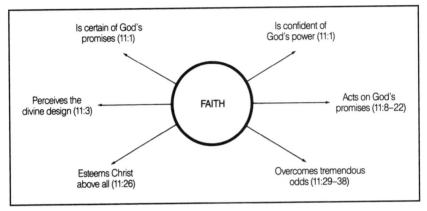

* Chart adapted from *Nelson's Complete Book of Bible Maps & Charts: Old and New Testaments*. © 1993, 1996 Thomas Nelson, Inc., Nashville, Tennessee. All rights reserved. Used by permission.

The Hall of Fame of Faith*

The hall of fame of the Scriptures is located in Hebrews 11 and records those who willingly took God at His word even when there was nothing to cling to but His promise.

Person	Scripture Reference
Abel	Genesis 4:1-15; Matthew 23:35
Enoch	Genesis 5:18-24
Noah	Genesis 6:5–9:18
Abraham	Genesis 11:31–25:10
Jonah	Jonah 1:1–4:11
Isaac	Genesis 22:1–35:29
Jacob	Genesis 25:21–50:13; Hosea 12:3-6
Joseph	Genesis 30:22–50:26
Moses' parents	Exodus 2:1-9
Moses	Exodus 2:1–Deuteronomy 34:8
Rahab	Joshua 2:1-24; 6:17-25
Gideon	Judges 6:11–8:32
Barak	Judges 4:1-31
Samson	Judges 13:1–16:31
Jephthah	Judges 11:1–12:7
David	1 Samuel 17:12–1 Kings 2:1
Samuel	1 Samuel 1:19–25:1
The Prophets	Various

Section Three // **Other Products from** the voice™

An Excerpt from:

The Last Eyewitness: The Final Week

The Voice of Matthew

The Voice of Luke: Not Even Sandals

The Voice Revealed: The True Story of the Last Eyewitness

The Voice of Acts: The Dust Off Their Feet

The Voice from on High

John 13

¹Before the Passover festival began, Jesus was keenly aware that His hour had come to depart from this world and to return to the Father. From beginning to end, Jesus' days were marked by His love for His people. ²Before Jesus and His disciples gathered for dinner, the adversary filled Judas Iscariot's heart with plans of deceit and betrayal. ³Jesus, knowing that He had come from God and was going away to God, ⁴stood up from dinner and removed His outer garments. He then wrapped Himself in a towel, ⁵poured water in a basin, and began to wash the feet of the disciples, drying them with His towel.

Simon Peter	6	*(as Jesus approaches)* Lord, are You going to wash my feet?
Jesus	7	Peter, you don't realize what I am doing, but you will understand later.
Peter	8	You will not wash my feet, now or ever!

I have to interrupt the story so you can get the whole picture. Can you imagine what it would feel like to have Jesus (the creative force behind the entire cosmos) wash your feet?

Have you ever been in a gathering where a rich and powerful person offers to fill your glass? You are thinking, "I should do this myself. How is it that someone of your stature would be willing to serve me?" But later you find yourself serving those who would view you as rich and powerful in the same ways that you were

Jesus Washing the Disciples' Feet

served. Multiply that experience by thousands, and you will have a small glimpse of this powerful expression.

My life changed that day; there was a new clarity about how I was supposed to live. I saw the world in a totally new way. The dirt, grime, sin, pain, rebellion, and torment around me were no longer an impediment to the spiritual path—it was the path.

Where I saw pain and filth, I found an opportunity to extend God's kingdom through an expression of love, humility, and service. This simple act is a metaphor for the lens that Christ gives us to see the cosmos. He sees the people, the world He created—which He loves—He sees the filth, the corruption in the world that torments us. His mission is to cleanse those whom He loves from the horrors that torment them. This is His redemptive work with feet, families, disease, famine, and our hearts.

So many of you have missed the heart of the gospel and Christ's example. When you see sin exposed in people, you shake your head and think how sad it is. Or worse you look down at these people for their rejection of God, lack of understanding, and poor morals. This is not the way of Christ. When Christ saw disease, He saw the opportunity to heal. Where He saw sin, He saw a chance to forgive and redeem. When He saw dirty feet, He saw a chance to wash them.

What do you see when you wander through the market, along the streets, on the beaches, and through the slums? Are you disgusted? Or do you seize the opportunity to expand God's reign of love in the cosmos? This is what Jesus did. The places we avoid, Jesus seeks. Now I must digress to tell a bit of the story from long before. I remember Him leading our little group of disciples into one of the most wretched places I have ever seen. It was a series of pools where the crippled and diseased would gather in hopes of being healed. The stench was unbearable, and no sane person would march into an area littered with wretched bodies and communicable diseases. We followed Him reluctantly as He approached a crippled man on his mat and said to him, "Are you here in this place hoping to be healed?" The disabled man responded, "Kind Sir, I wait, like all of these people for the waters to stir, but I cannot walk. If I am to be healed by the waters, some-one must carry me into the pool. So, the answer to Your question is yes—but I cannot be healed here unless someone will help me. Without a helping hand, someone else beats me to the water each time it is stirred." So, Jesus said, "Stand up, carry your mat and walk." At the moment Jesus uttered these words a healing energy coursed through the man and returned life to his limbs—he stood and walked for the first time in thirty-eight years (5:6-9).

It was not clear to us whether or not this man deserved this miracle. In fact, many of the disciples were disgusted by his lack of gratefulness and that he implicated Jesus to some of the Jewish authorities for healing him on the Sabbath. But God's grace is not earned; it is a beautiful gift to all of us.

When Jesus washed our feet He made an announcement to all who follow His path that life would not be about comfort, health, prosperity, and selfish pursuit.

I have gotten away from the story that was barely started. Let me back up and start almost from the beginning of the story again.

John 13

Simon Peter	6	*(as Jesus approaches)* Lord, are You going to wash my feet?
Jesus	7	Peter, you don't realize what I am doing, but you will understand later.
Peter	8	You will not wash my feet, now or ever!

Jesus		If I don't wash you, you will have nothing to do with Me.
Peter	9	Then wash me but don't stop with my feet. Cleanse my hands and head as well.
Jesus	10	Listen, anyone who has bathed is clean all over except for the feet. But I tell you this, not all of you are clean.

[11]He knew the one with plans of betraying Him, which is why He said, "not all of you are clean." [12]After washing their feet and picking up His garments, He reclined at the table again.

Jesus		Do you understand what I have done to you?
	13	You call Me Teacher and Lord, and truly, that is
	14	who I am. So, if your Lord and Teacher washes your feet, then you should wash one another's
	15	feet. I am your example; keep doing what I do.
	16	I tell you the truth: an apostle is not greater than the master. Those who are sent are not greater
	17	than the One who sends them. If you know these things, and if you put them into practice,
	18	you will find happiness. I am not speaking about all of you. I know whom I have chosen, but let the Scripture be fulfilled that says, "The very same man who eats My bread with Me, will
	19	stab Me in the back." Assuredly, I tell you these truths before they happen, so that when it all
	20	transpires you will believe that I am. I tell you the truth: anyone who accepts the ones I send accepts Me. In turn, the ones who accept Me, also accept the One who sent Me.

²¹Jesus was becoming visibly distressed.

Jesus | I tell you the truth: one of you will betray Me.

²²The disciples began to stare at one another, wondering who was the unfaithful disciple. ²³One disciple in particular, who was loved by Jesus, reclined next to Him at the table. ²⁴Peter motioned to the disciple at Jesus' side.

Peter | *(to the beloved disciple)* Find out who the betrayer is.

Beloved Disciple | 25 | *(leaning in to Jesus)* Lord, who is it?

Jesus | 26 | I will dip a piece of bread in My cup and give it to the one who will betray Me.

He dipped one piece in the cup and gave it to Judas, the son of Simon Iscariot. ²⁷After this occurred, Satan entered into Judas.

Jesus | *(to Judas)* Make haste, and do what you are going to do.

²⁸No one understood Jesus' instructions to Judas. ²⁹Because Judas carried the money, some thought he was being instructed to buy the necessary items for the feast, or give some money to the poor. ³⁰So Judas took his piece of bread and departed into the night.
³¹Upon Judas' departure, Jesus spoke:

Jesus | | Now the Son of Man will be glorified as God is
 | 32 | glorified in Him. If God's glory is in Him, His glory is also in God. The moment of this astounding

	33	glory is imminent. My children, My time here is brief. You will be searching for Me, and as I told the Jews, "You cannot go where I am going."
	34	So, I give you a new command: Love each other deeply and fully. Remember the ways that I have loved you, and demonstrate your love for
	35	others in those same ways. Everyone will know you as followers of Christ if you demonstrate your love to others.
Simon Peter	36	Lord, where are You going?
Jesus		Peter, you cannot come with Me now, but later you will join Me.
Peter	37	Why can't I go now? I'll give my life for You!
Jesus	38	Will you really give your life for Me? I tell you the truth: you will deny Me three times before the rooster crows.

Ultimately, Peter was telling the truth. He was more than willing to lay down his life. But none of us understood the magnitude of the persecution and hatred that was about to be unleashed on all of us. You ask me, "Did that change the way you led and treated people in your community or outside of it? Some of us think you have an ax to grind with the Jews. What connection did this pattern of living have with Jesus' command to love? How can you reconcile your angst against the Jews and this command Christ gave you to love?"

Matthew

HEROD AND JOHN; JESUS FEEDS 5,000

¹At this time, the ruler *of Galilee* was Herod *Antipas.* He began to hear reports about all that Jesus was doing.

²*Like the people of Nazareth,* Herod wondered where Jesus' power came from.

Herod *(to his servants)*	He must be John the Teacher who washed ceremonially,* raised from the dead; thus His power.

> *H*erod was quite concerned with the attention that John the Teacher was receiving, but he didn't want to spend precious political capital killing a reputed holy man. On top of that, Jesus was beginning to create an even greater problem for Herod.

³⁻⁵Herod's brother Philip had married a woman named Herodias, *who eventually married Herod.* John denounced Herod's marriage to her as adulterous. Herod was incensed *(not to mention a little fearful)* and wanted to kill John, but he knew the people considered John a prophet. Instead, he bound John and put him in jail.

⁶⁻⁷*There John sat until* Herod's birthday. On that night, *Salome,* Herodias's daughter *by Philip,* came and danced for her stepfather and all his birthday guests. Herod so enjoyed her dancing that he vowed to give her whatever she wanted.

14:2 Literally, John who immersed, to show repentance

Salome *(after whispering with her mother)*	[8]Bring me the head of John the Teacher and Prophet,* displayed on a platter.

> *T*his was not what Herod had expected—he'd imagined his step-daughter might ask for a necklace or maybe a slave.

[9]Herod still thought it unwise to kill John, but *because he had made such a show of his promise*—because he had actually sworn an oath and *because the scene was playing out* in front of *the watchful eyes* of so many guests—Herod felt bound *to give his stepdaughter what she wanted.* [10]And so he sent orders to the prison to have John beheaded, [11]and there was his head, displayed on a platter, given first to *Salome* and then passed on to her mother.

[12]John's disciples went to the prison, got John's body, and buried him. Then they went to tell Jesus.

[13]When Jesus learned what had happened, He got on a boat and went away to spend some time in a private place. The crowds, of course, followed Jesus, on foot from their cities. [14]*Though Jesus wanted solitude,* when He saw the crowds, He had compassion on them, and He healed the sick *and the lame.* [15]At evening-time, Jesus' disciples came to Him.

Disciples	We're in a fairly remote place, and it is getting late; *the crowds will get hungry for supper.* Send them away so they have time to get back to the village and get something to eat.
Jesus	[16]They don't need to go back to the village in order to eat supper. Give them something to eat here.

14:8 Literally, John who immersed, to show repentance

Disciples	[17]*But we don't have enough food.* We only have five rounds *of flatbread* and two fish.
Jesus	[18]Bring the bread and the fish to Me.

So the disciples brought Him the five rounds of flatbread, and the two fish, [19]and Jesus told the people to sit down on the grass. He took the bread and the fish, He looked up to heaven, He gave thanks, and then He broke the bread. Jesus gave the bread to the disciples, and the disciples gave the bread to the people; [20]everyone ate and was satisfied. *When everyone had eaten,* the disciples picked up 12 baskets *of crusts and broken pieces of bread and crumbs. Not only was there enough, but there was an abundance.* [21]There were 5,000 men there, not to mention all the women and children.

[22]Immediately, Jesus made the disciples get into the boat and go on to the other side of the sea while He dismissed the crowd. [23]Then, after the crowd had gone, Jesus went up to a mountaintop alone (*as He had intended from the start*). As evening descended, He stood alone on the mountain, praying. [24]The boat was in the water, some distance from land, buffeted and pushed around by waves and wind.

[25]Deep in the night, *when He had concluded His prayers,* Jesus walked out on the water to His disciples *in their boat.* [26]The disciples saw a figure moving toward them and were terrified.

Disciple	It's a ghost!
Another Disciple	A ghost? What will we do?
Jesus	[27] Be still. It is I. You have nothing to fear.
Peter	[28]Lord, if it is really You, then command me to meet You on the water.

Jesus | [29]*Indeed,* come.

Peter stepped out of the boat onto the water and began walking toward Jesus. [30]But when he remembered how strong the wind was, his courage caught in his throat and he began to sink.

Peter | Master, save me!

[31]Immediately, Jesus reached for Peter and caught him.

Jesus | O you of little faith. Why did you doubt *and dance back and forth between following* Me *and heeding fear?*

[32]Then Jesus and Peter climbed in the boat together, and the wind became still. [33]And the disciples worshiped Him.

Disciples | Truly You are the Son of God.

[34]All together, Jesus and the disciples crossed *to the other side of the sea.* They landed at Gennesaret, *an area famous for its princely gardens.* [35]The people of Gennesaret recognized Jesus, and they spread word of His arrival all over the countryside. People brought the sick *and wounded* to Him [36]and begged Him for permission to touch the fringes of His robe. Everyone who touched Him was healed.

FOR THOSE WHO LOVE GOD

*W*hat are your assumptions as you begin this amazing document? What do you assume about Luke as an author—his motives, his agenda, his assumptions? Any constructive experience of reading involves an amazing interaction so complex that it's a wonder it ever works at all. First, there are readers across time and space, each reading with certain questions, certain assumptions, and a certain worldview. Then there's an author, located in another specific time and place, embedded in his own context and worldview. The author and the readers also come from communities or traditions—groups of people who share their basic worldview and who teach them to think, write, read, and respond in certain ways.

In all my years of reading (and writing), I've concluded that we as readers have the obligation to try to enter the writer's world, to understand him on his own terms and in his own context, rather than requiring him to enter ours (something he can't do!). That means that we need to try to imagine Luke's world. Fortunately, we have Luke's sequel to this Gospel to help us understand more about him. (It's called the Acts of the Apostles, and the two documents shed light on each other.) Tradition tells us that Luke is a physician, active in the early church in the years around A.D. 60. He travels widely with the emissary Paul; so he is a sort of cosmopolitan person, multicultural in his sensitivities, understanding both Jewish culture and the broader Greco-Roman culture of the Roman Empire. As a physician, he is more educated than the average person of his day, but I think you'll be impressed with his ability to relate to common people—and especially his skill as a storyteller. Remember that Luke isn't presenting us with a theological treatise (as good and important as theological treatises may be); he's telling us the story of Jesus, gathered from many eyewitnesses. Based on the intended audience of his book (Theophilus—literally, God-lover), we can assume he wants to help people who love God to love Him even more by knowing what He has done through Jesus.

¹⁻³For those who love God, several other people have already written accounts of what God has been bringing to completion among us, using the reports of the original eyewitnesses, those who were there from the start to witness the fulfillment of prophecy. Like those other servants who have recorded the messages, I present to you my carefully researched, orderly account of these new teachings. ⁴I want you to know that you can fully rely on the things you have been taught *about Jesus, God's Anointed One.*

⁵*To understand the life of Jesus, I must first give you some background history, events that occurred when* Herod ruled Judea *for the Roman Empire.* Zacharias was serving as a priest *in the temple in Jerusalem* those days as his fathers had before him. He was a member of the priestly division of Abijah *(a grandson of Aaron who innovated temple practices),* and his wife, Elizabeth, was of the priestly lineage of Aaron, *Moses' brother.* ⁶They were good and just people in God's sight, walking with integrity in the Lord's ways and laws. ⁷Yet they had this sadness. Due to Elizabeth's infertility, they were childless,

and at this time, they were both quite old—*well past normal childbearing years.*

*I*n the time of Jesus, Jewish life was centered in the temple in Jerusalem. The temple was staffed by religious professionals, what we might refer to as "clergy" today, called priests. They were responsible for the temple's activities—which included receiving religious pilgrims and their sacrifices (cattle, sheep, goats, and doves). Animal sacrifices sound strange to us—we often associate them with some kind of extremist cult. But in the ancient world, they were quite common. It may help, in trying to understand animal sacrifices, to remember that the slaughter of animals was a daily experience in the ancient world; it was part of any meal that included meat. So perhaps we should think of the sacrifice of animals as, first and foremost, a special meal. This meal brings together the Jewish family from near and far, seeking to affirm their connection to the one true and living God. Their gift of animals was their contribution to the meal. (The priests, by the way, were authorized to use the meat for the sustenance of their families.)

The presentation of the blood and meat of these sacrifices was accompanied by a number of prescribed rituals, performed by priests wearing prescribed ornamental clothing, according to a prescribed schedule. As the story continues, we see these solemn rituals interrupted in a most unprecedented way.

⁸One day, Zacharias was chosen to perform his priestly duties in God's presence, according to the temple's normal schedule and

routine. ⁹He had been selected from all the priests by the customary procedure of casting lots *for a once-in-a-lifetime opportunity* to enter the sacred precincts of the temple. There he burned sweet incense, ¹⁰while outside a large crowd of people prayed. ¹¹*Suddenly, Zacharias realized he was not alone:* a messenger of the Lord was there with him. The messenger stood just to the right of the altar of incense. ¹²Zacharias was shocked and afraid, ¹³but the messenger reassured him.

Messenger | Zacharias, calm down! Don't be afraid!

*A*gain and again, when people encounter God (or when they receive a message from God, often through a vision of a heavenly messenger), their first response is terror; and so they need to be calmed down before they can receive the message. We might think Zacharias shouldn't be surprised to hear from God; after all, he's a priest working in the temple. But priests didn't normally hear from God. Those who heard from God were called prophets, not priests.

Priests worked "the family business," so to speak. One became a priest by being born in a priestly family line. Prophets, on the other hand, arose unpredictably. Prophets had no special credentials except the message they carried. So Zacharias had no reason to believe his duties would be interrupted in this way.

Often in the biblical story, when people receive a message from God, after getting over the initial shock, they start asking questions. They push back; they doubt. However, when the word of the Lord comes to people, it doesn't turn them into unthinking zombies or robots; it doesn't override their individuality or capacity to think. Perhaps many of us in some way hear the voice of the Lord, but we don't realize it because we're expecting lightning flashes and a voice with a lot of reverb, a voice so overpowering that we are incapable of questioning and doubting it.

Messenger | Zacharias, your prayers have been heard. Your wife is going to have a son, and you will name him John. [14]He will bring you great joy and happiness—and many will share your joy at John's birth.

[15]This son of yours will be a great man in God's sight. He will not drink alcohol in any form; *instead of alcoholic spirits*, he will be filled with the Holy Spirit from the time he is in his mother's womb. [16]*Here is his mission: he will stop many of the children of Israel in their misguided paths, and* he'll turn them around to follow the path to the Lord their God instead.

[17]Do you remember the prophecy about someone to come in the spirit and power of the prophet Elijah; someone who will turn the hearts of the parents back to their children;* someone who will turn the hearts of the disobedient to the mind-set of the just and good? Your son is the one who will fulfill this prophecy: he will be the Lord's forerunner, the one who will prepare the people and make them ready for God.

1:17 Malachi 4:5-6

*W*e mentioned that Luke was a master storyteller, so we've decided to contextualize his method of storytelling to our own culture in some creative ways. First, we'll highlight dialogue (as you'll see we do in this episode), rendering Luke's account in the form of a screenplay. Second, from time to time, we'll have Luke say, "Picture this," or "Imagine this." Then we'll use present tense to help you enter the story imaginatively, as if you were there yourself.

Zacharias | [18]How can I be sure of what you're telling me? I am an old man, and my wife is far past the normal age for women to bear children. *This is hard to believe!*

Messenger
(sternly) | [19]I am Gabriel, the messenger who inhabits God's presence. I was sent here to talk with you and bring you this good news. [20]Because you didn't believe my message, you will not be able to talk—not another word—until you experience the fulfillment of my words.

[21]Meanwhile, the crowd at the temple wondered why Zacharias hadn't come out of the sanctuary yet. It wasn't normal for the priest to be delayed so long. [22]When at last he came out, *it was clear from his face something had happened in there.* He was making signs with his hands to give the blessing, but he couldn't speak. They realized he had seen some sort of vision. [23]When his time on duty at the temple came to an end, he went back home to his wife. [24]Shortly after his return, Elizabeth became pregnant. She avoided public contact for the next five months.

Elizabeth | 25I have lived with the disgrace of being barren for all these years. Now God has looked on me with favor. When I go out in public *with my baby*, I will not be disgraced any longer.

26Six months later in Nazareth, a city in *the rural province of* Galilee, the heavenly messenger Gabriel made another appearance. This time, the messenger was sent by God 27to meet with a virgin named Mary, who was engaged to a man named Joseph, a descendant of King David himself. 28The messenger entered her home.

Messenger | Greetings! You are favored, and the Lord is with you! [Among all women on the earth you have been blessed.]*

29The heavenly messenger's words baffled Mary, and she wondered what type of greeting this was.

Messenger | 30Mary, don't be afraid. You have found favor with God. 31Listen, you are going to become pregnant. You will have a Son, and you must name Him "Liberation," *or* Jesus.* 32Jesus will become the greatest among men. He will be known as the Son of the Highest God. God will give Him the throne of His ancestor David, 33and He will reign over the covenant family of Jacob forever.

1:28 The earliest manuscripts omit this portion.
1:31 Through the naming of Jesus, God is speaking prophetically about the role Jesus will play in our salvation.

*M*y name is John. My father's name was Zebedee. We made our living by fishing on the Sea of Galilee. I am the last eyewitness to the life of Jesus. All the rest are gone; some long gone. Many died years ago, tragically young, the victims of Roman cruelty and persecution. For some reason, Jesus chose me to live to be an old man. In fact, some in my community have taken to calling me "the elder."

I am the inspiration behind the Fourth Gospel. These are my stories, recorded, told to you by my disciples. I'm proud of what they have done. Me? I've never done much writing. But the story is truly mine.

You see my hands. They've been hurting for the past 20 years now. I couldn't hold a pen even if I wanted to. Not that I was ever good at writing. I was a fisherman, so my hands were calloused. I could tie ropes, mend nets, and pull the oars, but never make a decent *xi* (Greek letter). So we used secretaries when we wanted to write. There was always a bright young man around it seems, ready to take a letter or help us put pen to papyrus.

My eyes are too weak to read anymore. I can't remember the last time I could see well enough to read a letter or even see the inscriptions. So one of the brothers (I call them my "little children") reads to me. They are all very gracious to me in my old age, compiling my stories, bringing me food, laughing at my jokes, and caring for my most intimate needs. Time is taking its toll on me though. I rarely have the energy to tell the old stories and preach entire sermons. Instead, I simply remind them of the Liberating King's most vital command, saying as loudly as I can, "Little children, love one another."

Jesus had this group of guys. He called us "the twelve." We traveled with Him, spent time with Him, ate with Him, and listened to Him talk about God's kingdom. We watched Him perform miracles. These weren't the tricks like you see in the market or attempts at magic you hear about at shrines. These were what I call "signs." Something was breaking into our darkness. These signs pointed to a greater reality most people didn't even know was there. In the other Gospels, they call them "miracles" or "works of power." We've decided to tell you about select signs because these, more than any, revealed the true glory of this man.

Jesus wanted us to be His family, a different kind of community. We figured it out later. By calling us "the twelve," Jesus was remembering the original twelve tribes of Israel while creating a new people of God. God was doing something new, like the prophets had promised. We were living at the center of history. From now on, everything would be different. This made us feel special, proud, and sometimes arrogant. We'd sometimes jockey for Jesus' attention. Even within the twelve some were closer to Jesus. He had this "inner circle" of sorts. I was part of it. Peter, Andrew, James, and I were with Jesus at times when the other fellows had to stay behind. I'm not sure why He picked me. Because of that, I knew He loved me and I would have a special place with Him.

Jesus also had other students. Not all of them stayed. Some came, and some went. I don't really know how many people in all. One time He sent out 70 of us to proclaim the good news and heal in His name. He even let women be His students. Most people don't know this, but women were among those who helped support us financially.[1] At a time when people said it was a shame for a man to be supported by women, Jesus took their help and took it gladly. But there were no women among the twelve. That was only right. In our day, women didn't travel with men who were not family. Scandal was always swirling around Jesus; He didn't want or need to fight that battle.

I've outlived all the rest of the twelve and His other followers. I can't tell you how lonely it is to be the last person

---

[1] Luke 8:3

with a memory, some would even say a fuzzy memory, of what Jesus looked like, the sound of His voice, the manner of His walk, the penetrating look in His eyes. All I can do is tell my story.

Others have written accounts of what happened among us. The other Gospels have faithfully portrayed the public Jesus. But I feel compelled to tell the story of the private Jesus. The others show us how Jesus preached and dealt with the multitudes. But I still remember the small group time with Jesus and the conversations He had with Nicodemus, the Samaritan woman, and the man born blind—I don't remember his name.

The other Gospels tell the tragedy and injustice of Jesus' death. Here was the single greatest man in history who was falsely accused; who was dragged before corrupt priests and a cruel Roman governor. He was condemned to death and crucified in a most hideous manner. On a human level, Jesus' arrest, condemnation, and crucifixion were tragedies of epic proportions. But the more this old man thinks about what happened, the more I understand now that Jesus' death was His greatest hour. Things seemed to spin out of control so quickly. One minute we were celebrating the Passover together in the upper room; the next we were running for our lives! I'm not sure who was to blame for what happened to Jesus. Envious priests? The Roman governor? But, in fact, He was in complete control. That's why I say the hour of His death was the hour of His greatest glory. That's why I think that when Jesus was lifted up on the cross, He became the means by which all people can come to God. The most vivid memory that lingers in this old man's mind is of Jesus up there on the cross. I can still see it like it was yesterday. His body—hanging halfway between heaven and earth, embracing the world—bridged the gap between God and humanity.

Now I want to be very clear. This is my story, but unlike

what you hear from most storytellers, this is completely true. I am giving you the testimony of an eyewitness. And like my brother disciples, I will swear upon my life that it is true.

John 1

[1]Before time itself was measured, the Voice was speaking. The Voice was and is God. [2]This *celestial* Voice remained ever present with the Creator; [3]His speech shaped the entire cosmos. *Immersed in the practice of creating,* all things that exist were birthed in Him. [4]His breath filled all things with a living, breathing light. [5]Light that thrives in the depths of darkness, *blazing through murky bottoms.* It cannot, and will not, be quenched.

[6]A man named John, who was sent by God, *was the first to clearly articulate the source of this unquenchable Light.* [7]This wanderer, *John who ritually cleansed,** put in plain words the *elusive mystery of the Divine* Light that all might believe through him. *Because John spoke with power, many believed in the Light. Others wondered whether he might be the Light,* [8]but John was not the Light. He merely pointed to the Light; *and in doing so, he invited the entire creation to hear the Voice.*

[9]The true Light, who shines upon the heart of everyone, was coming into the cosmos. [10]*He does not call out from a distant place but draws near.* He enters our world, a world He made *and speaks clearly,* yet His creation did not recognize Him. [11]*Though the Voice utters only truth,* His own people, *who have heard the Voice before,* rebuff this inner calling and refuse to listen. [12]But those who *hear and* trust the beckoning of the Divine Voice and embrace Him, they shall be reborn as children of God, [13]He bestows this birthright not by human

---

* 1:7 Literally, immersed, to show repentance

power or initiative but by God's will. *Because we are born of this world, we can only be reborn to God by accepting His call.*

[14]The Voice *that had been an enigma in the heavens chose to* become human and live surrounded by His creations. We have seen Him. Undeniable splendor enveloped Him—the one true Son of God—*evidenced in* the perfect balance of grace and truth. [15]John, *the wanderer* who testified of the Voice, introduced Him. "This is the one I've been telling you is coming. He is much greater than I because He existed *long* before me." [16]Through this man we all receive *gifts of* grace beyond our imagination. *He is the Voice of God.* [17]You see, Moses gave us rules to live by, but Jesus the Liberating King offered the gifts of grace and truth *which make life worth living.* [18]God, unseen until now, is revealed in the Voice, God's only Son, *straight from* the Father's heart.

> *B*efore Jesus came along, many thought John the Immerser might be the Liberating King. But when Jesus appeared in the wilderness, John pointed us to Him. The Immerser knew his place in God's redemptive plan. John the Immerser was a man sent from God, but Jesus is the Voice of God. John rejected any messianic claim outright. Jesus, though, accepted it with a smile, but only from a few of us—at least at first. Don't get me wrong, John was important, but he wasn't the Liberating King. He preached repentance. He told everybody to get ready for One greater to come along. The One who comes will immerse us in fire and power, he said. John even told some of his followers to leave him and go follow Jesus.

[19]The words of the Immerser were *gaining attention,* and many had questions, including Jewish religious leaders from Jerusalem. [28]Their entourage approached John in Bethany just beyond the Jordan River while he was cleansing[*] followers in water, *and bombarded him with questions:[*]*

---

* 1:28 Literally, immersing, to show repentance
* 1:28 Verse 28 has been inserted here to help retain the continuity of events.

Religious Leaders: Who are you?

John the Immerser: [20]I'm not the Liberator, *if that is what you are asking.*

Religious Leaders: [21]*Your words sound familiar, like a prophet's.* Is that how we should address you? Are you the Prophet Elijah?

John the Immerser: No, I am not Elijah.

Religious Leaders: Are you the Prophet *Moses told us would come?*

John the Immerser: No.

They continued to press John, unsatisfied with the lack of information.

Religious Leaders: [22]Then tell us who you are and what you are about because everyone is asking us, *especially the Pharisees,* and we must prepare an answer.

[23]John replied with the words of Isaiah:

John the Immerser: *Listen!* I am a voice calling out in the wilderness.

Straighten out the road for the Lord. *He's on His way.*[*]

[24-25]Then, some priests who were sent by the Pharisees started in on him again.

Religious Leaders: How can you *travel the countryside* cleansing[*] people from their sins if you are not the Liberator or Elijah or the Prophet?

John the Immerser: [26]Cleansing[*] with water is what I do, but the One *whom I speak of, whom we all await,* is standing among you and you have no idea who He is. [27]Though He comes after me, I am not even worthy to unlace His sandals.[*]

---

* 1:23 Isaiah 40:3
* 1:24-25 Literally, immersing, to show repentance
* 1:26 Literally, immersion, to show repentance
* 1:27 Verse 28 has been moved before verse 20 to retain the continuity of events.

The mystery of Jesus' identity occupied us and will occupy generations of believers for centuries to come. As we journeyed with Him, it gradually became clearer who this man was, where He came from, and how His existence would profoundly affect the rest of human history. The question of "Who is this man?" was not answered overnight.

²⁹The morning after *this conversation as John is going about his business*, he sees *the Voice*, Jesus, coming toward him. *In eager astonishment* he shouts out:

John the Immerser: Look! *This man is more than He seems!* He is the Lamb sent from God, *the sacrifice* to erase the sins of the world! ³⁰He is the One I have been saying will come after me, who existed long before me and is much greater than I. ³¹*No one here* recognized Him—myself included. I came ritually cleansing* with water so that He might be revealed to Israel. ³²⁻³³And, just as the One who sent me told me, I knew who He was the moment I saw the Spirit come down upon Him as a dove and seal itself to Him. Now, He will cleanse* with the Holy Spirit. ³⁴I give my oath that everything I have seen is true. *If you don't believe now, keep listening.* He is *the Voice*, the Son of God!

³⁵⁻³⁶The day after, John *saw Him again as he* was visiting with two of his disciples. As Jesus walked by, he announced again:

John the Immerser: Do you see Him? This man is the Lamb of God; *He will be God's sacrifice to cleanse our sin.*

³⁷At that moment the two disciples began to follow Jesus, ³⁸⁻³⁹who turned back to them, saying:

Jesus: What is it that you want?

---

* 1:31 Literally, immersion, to show repentance
* 1:32-33 Literally, immerse

Two Disciples: We'd like to know where You are staying. Teacher, *may we remain at Your side today?*
Jesus: Come and see. *Follow Me, and we will camp together.*

It was about four o'clock in the afternoon *when they met Jesus.* They came and they saw where He was staying *but they got more than they imagined.* They remained with Him the rest of the day *and followed Him for the rest of their lives.* [40-41]One of these new disciples, Andrew, rushed to find his brother Simon and tell him they had found the Christ, the Liberating King, *the One who will heal the world.* [42]As Andrew approached with Simon, Jesus looked into him.

Jesus: Your name is Simon, and your father is called John. But from this day forward you will be known as Peter,[*] the rock.

[43-44]The next day Jesus set out to Galilee; and when He came upon Philip, He invited him to join them,

Jesus: Follow Me.

Philip, like Andrew and Peter, came from a town called Bethsaida *and he decided to make the journey with Him.* [45]Philip found Nathanael, *a friend, and burst in with excitement*:

Philip: We have found the One. Moses wrote about Him in the Law; all the prophets spoke of the day when He would come, and now He is here—His name is Jesus, son of Joseph *the carpenter*, and He comes from Nazareth.
Nathanael: [46]How can anything good come from *a place like* Nazareth?
Philip: Come with me. See *and hear* for yourself.

[47]As they approached, Jesus saw Nathanael coming.

Jesus: Look closely and you will see an Israelite who is a truth-teller.

---

[*] 1:42 Aramaic *Cephas*

Nathanael: [48]How would You know this about me? *We have never met.*

Jesus: *I have been watching you* before Philip invited you here. *Earlier in the day* you were enjoying *the shade and fruit of* the fig tree. I saw you then.

Nathanael: [49]Teacher, *I am sorry—forgive me.* You are the One—God's own Son and Israel's King.

Jesus: [50]Nathanael, if all it takes for you to believe is My telling you I saw you under the fig tree, then what you will see later shall astound you. *The miracles you will witness are greater than your imagination can comprehend.* [51]I tell you the truth: *before our journey is complete,* you will see the heavens standing open while heavenly messengers ascend and descend, *swirling* around the Son of Man.

Chapter 2

[1-2]Three days after *the disciples encountered Jesus for the first time,* they were all invited to celebrate a wedding feast in Cana of Galilee together with Mary, the mother of Jesus. [3]While they were celebrating, the wine ran out and Jesus' mother hurried over to her son.

Mary: *The host stands on the brink of embarrassment; there are many guests and* there is no more wine.

Jesus: [4]Dear woman, is it our problem *they miscalculated when buying wine and inviting guests*? My time has not arrived.

[5]*But Mary sensed the time was near. So in a way that only a mother can,* she turned to the servants.

Mary: Do whatever my son tells you.

A TASTE OF THE KINGDOM

¹When the holy day of Pentecost came _50 days after Passover_, they were gathered together in one place.

Picture yourself among the disciples: ²A sound roars from the sky without warning, the roar of a violent wind, and the whole house where you are gathered reverberates with the sound. ³Then a flame appears, dividing into smaller flames and spreading from one person to the next. ⁴All the apostles are filled with the Holy Spirit and begin speaking in languages they've never spoken, as the Spirit empowers them.

⁵_Because of the holiday,_ there were devoted Jews staying as pilgrims in Jerusalem from every nation under the sun. ⁶They heard the sound, and a crowd gathered. They were amazed because each of them could hear the group speaking in their native languages. ⁷They were shocked and amazed by this.

Pilgrims | Just a minute. Aren't all of these people Galileans? ⁸How in the world do we all hear our native languages being spoken? ⁹_Look_—there are Parthians _here_, and Medes, Elamites, Mesopotamians, and Judeans, residents of Cappadocia, Pontus, and Asia, ¹⁰Phrygians and Pamphylians, Egyptians and Libyans from Cyrene, Romans including both Jews by birth and converts, ¹¹Cretans, and Arabs. We're each, in our own languages, hearing these people talk about God's powerful deeds.

¹²Their amazement became confusion as they wondered,

Pilgrims | What does this mean?

Skeptics | ¹³It doesn't mean anything. They're all drunk on some fresh wine!

*N*o matter who you were or what you may have seen, this miraculous sign of God's kingdom would have astounded you. The followers of Jesus were not known as people who drank too much wine with breakfast, but this unusual episode required some kind of explanation. Unfortunately, we can't comprehend or express what transpired on Pentecost. But this was not a novelty performance; rather, it was a taste of the kingdom of God.

¹⁴As the twelve stood together, Peter shouted to the crowd,

Peter | Men of Judea and all who are staying here in Jerusalem, listen. I want you to understand: ¹⁵these people aren't drunk as you may think. Look, it's only nine o'clock in the morning! ¹⁶*No, this isn't drunkenness; this is the fulfillment of the prophecy of Joel.* ¹⁷*Hear what God says!*

In the last days, I will offer My Spirit to humanity as a libation.
Your children will boldly speak *the word of the Lord.*

Young warriors will see visions, and your elders will
dream dreams.

¹⁸Yes, in those days I shall offer My Spirit to all servants,
Both male and female [and they will boldly speak the
word of the Lord].

¹⁹And in the heaven above and on the earth below,
I shall give signs *of impending judgment*: blood, fire, and
clouds of smoke.

²⁰The sun will become a void of darkness, and the moon
will become blood.

Then the great and dreadful day of the Lord will arrive,

²¹And everyone who pleads using the name of the Lord
Will be liberated *into God's freedom and peace*.*

²²All of you Israelites, listen to my message: it's about
Jesus of Nazareth, a Man whom God authenticated for
you by performing in your presence powerful deeds,
wonders, and signs through Him, just as you yourselves
know. ²³This *Man, Jesus*, who came into your hands by
God's sure plan and advanced knowledge, you nailed to
a cross and killed in collaboration with lawless Gentiles.
²⁴But God raised Jesus and unleashed Him from the ago-
nizing birth-pains of death, for death could not possibly
keep Jesus in its power. ²⁵David spoke *of Jesus'
resurrection*, saying:

The Lord is ever present with me. I will not live in
fear or abandon my calling because He guides my

2:21 Joel 2:28-32

right hand. [26]My heart is glad; my soul rejoices; my body is safe. Who could want for more? [27]You will not abandon me to experience the suffering of a miserable afterlife. Nor leave me to rot alone. [28]Instead, You direct me on a path that leads to a beautiful life. As I walk with You the pleasures are never-ending, and I know true joy and contentment.*

[29] My fellow Israelites, I can say without question that David our ancestor died and was buried, and his tomb is with us today. [30]*David wasn't speaking of himself;* he was speaking as a prophet. *He saw with prophetic insight* that God had made a solemn promise to him: God would put one of his descendants on His throne. [31]Here's what David was seeing in advance; here's what David was talking about—the Messiah, the Liberating King, would be resurrected. *Think of David's words about* Him not being abandoned to the place of the dead nor being left to decay in the grave. [32]*He was talking about* Jesus, the One God has raised, whom all of us have seen with our own eyes and announce to you today. [33]Since Jesus has been lifted to the right hand of God—*the highest place of authority and power*—and since Jesus has received the promise of the Holy Spirit from the Father, He has now poured out what you have seen and heard here today. [34]*Remember:* David couldn't have been speaking of himself rising to the heavens when he said, "The Lord God said to my Lord, the King,

---

³⁵"Sit here at My right hand, in the place of honor and power, and I will gather Your enemies together, lead them in on hands and knees, and You will rest Your feet on their backs.'"*

³⁶Everyone in Israel should now realize with certainty *what God has done*: God has made Jesus both Lord and Liberating King—this same Jesus whom you crucified.

³⁷When the people heard this, their hearts were pierced and they said to Peter and his fellow apostles,

Pilgrims | Our brothers, what should we do?

Peter | ³⁸Reconsider your lives; change your direction. Participate in the ceremonial washing* in the name of Jesus the Liberating King. Then your sins will be forgiven, and the gift of the Holy Spirit will be yours. ³⁹For the promise *of the Spirit* is for you, for your children, for all people—even those considered outsiders and outcasts—the Lord our God invites everyone to come to Him. Let God liberate you from this decaying culture!

Peter was pleading and offering many logical reasons to believe. ⁴¹Whoever made a place for his message in their hearts received the ceremonial washing*; in fact, that day alone, about 3,000 people joined the disciples.

2:35 Psalm 110:1
2:38 Literally, immersion, a rite of initiation and purification
2:41 Literally, immersion, a rite of initiation and purification

[42]The community continually committed themselves to learning what the apostles taught them, gathering for fellowship, breaking the bread, and praying. [43]Everyone felt a sense of awe because the apostles were doing many signs and wonders among them. [44]There was an intense sense of togetherness among all who believed; they shared all their material possessions in trust. [45]They sold any possessions and goods *that did not benefit the community* and used the money to help everyone in need. [46]They were unified as they worshiped at the temple day after day. In homes, they broke bread and shared meals with glad and generous hearts. [47]The new disciples praised God, and they enjoyed the goodwill of all the people of the city. Day after day the Lord added to their number everyone who was experiencing liberation.

Although this young and thriving church had no political influence, property, fame, or wealth, it was powerful. Its power was centered in living the gospel. The people valued one another more than any possessions. They came together as a large, passionate, healthy family where it was natural to pray and share all of life together. The kingdom of God was blossoming on earth as these lovers of God embraced the teachings of Christ. The church has since lost much of the beauty and appeal we see in Acts. It has become concerned with a desire for material possessions, cultural influence, and large congregations.

The Orchestra Waits with Anticipation (He Will Feed His Fold)

It is midnight. A deep silence blankets the earth. Stars pierce the darkness. A flock of sheep huddle together in a nearby field. A shepherd sits on a rock not far away, fighting sleep but maintaining a watchful eye. But one mischievous young lamb has strayed and lies asleep behind a rock on a nearby hill.

There's a frightful noise. The lamb awakens to the low growl of a wolf coming from the other side of the rock. The lamb cannot move—it is paralyzed with fear. The wolf shrieks; then there's silence. The lamb hooks his neck nervously around the rock, and standing there is the shepherd, its protector, who has killed the wolf and saved the lamb's life.

We are that mischievous lamb, and the Lord is our shepherd. He guides us through the meadows of life and protects us from the dangers that lurk at night. And, as long as we are not too far away from Him, He can clamp down on the snapping jaws of evil.

When Jesus calls Himself "the good shepherd," His disciples hear the echo of Psalm 23, "The Eternal One is my shepherd. . . ." But despite our romantic notions to the contrary, shepherding was not a noble profession in those days. So why would God choose to reveal Himself as a shepherd? It is because we are more like sheep than we'd like to admit and because He has committed Himself to serve, protect, and provide for us.

I am the good shepherd. The good shepherd lays down His life for the sheep *in His care*. The hired hand is not like the shepherd caring for His own sheep. When a wolf attacks, snatching and scattering the sheep, he runs for his life, leaving them *defenseless*. The hired hand runs because he works only for wages and does not care for the sheep. I am the good shepherd; I know My sheep, and My sheep know Me. As the Father knows Me, I know the Father; I will give My life for the sheep.[6]

Just as a true shepherd knows each one of his sheep by name, God knows every one of us. And, just as every sheep's life is important to a shepherd, so ours are important to the Good Shepherd.

Isaiah 40:1-5, 11

[1]"Comfort, comfort My people," says your God.

[2]"With the gentlest words, *tender and kind,*

Assure this city, this site of long-ago chosenness; speak unto Jerusalem
    their battles are over. The terror, the bloodshed, the horror
    of My punishing work is done.

This place has paid for its guilt; iniquity is pardoned;
    its term of incarceration is complete.
    It has endured double the punishment it was due."

[3]A voice is wailing, "In the wilderness,
    get it ready! Prepare the way,
    make it a straight shot. The Eternal One would have it so.
Straighten the way in the wandering desert
    to make the crooked road wide and straight for our God.

[6] John 10:11-15

⁴Where there are steep valleys, treacherous descents, raise the highway,
    lift it up;
    bring down the dizzying heights; humble them.
Fill the potholes and gullies, the rough places.
    Iron out the shoulders flat and wide.
⁵The Eternal One will be, really be, among us.
    The radiant glory *of the Lord* will be revealed.
    All flesh together will take it in.
    Believe it. None other than God, the Eternal One has spoken."

¹¹He will feed His fold like a shepherd;
    God will assure that we are safe and content.
He will gather together His lambs, *the weak and the wobbly ones*
    into His arms,
    carrying them close to His bosom.
And God tenderly leads those *burdened by care-taking*
    Like a shepherd leads the mothers of her lambs.

A recurring theme throughout Scripture is the ideal image that God relates to His people as a shepherd to his sheep. After the conquest of Jerusalem by the Babylonians, prophets and poets described God as the ultimate shepherd—guarding, providing, protecting, leading, and eventually herding His flock back to a New Jerusalem.

But the shepherd image can cut both ways. Israel and Judah often suffered exploitation and harm at the hands of wayward shepherds, harsh leaders more concerned about themselves than about their flock. But in Israel's critical moments, God's prophets envisioned another shepherd striding forward, Jesus our Liberating King. He would do more than shepherd us during this life; He would shepherd us for all the ages to come. And where would David's Son learn to shepherd us? From His Father and our God. The Lord is our shepherd.

Ezekiel 34:11-24

¹¹This is what the Lord, the Eternal One, says:

Eternal One

I will personally go out searching for My sheep. I will find them wherever they are, *and I will look after them.* ¹²In the same way that a shepherd seeks after, *cares for, and watches over* his scattered flock, so will I be the guardian of My congregation. I will be their Rescuer! *No matter where they have scattered, I will journey to find them.* I will bring them back from the places where they were scattered on that dark and cloudy day. *I will reach into hard-to-reach places; I will search out every secret pocket of the earth in order to save them from the darkness.* ¹³⁻¹⁴I will call them out from the nations and gather them from the countries, and I will bring them into their own land. I will give them *a sanctuary—a place where they can rest—*in the high mountain pastures and meadows of Israel. The mountain heights of Israel will be their nourishment, *their sanctuary.* I will introduce them to blooming pastures, where they can graze upon rich mountain lands *to* soothe their hunger. I will lead them along the banks of *glistening mountain* streams, *where they can drink clear, pure water and quench their thirst.*

¹⁵I will *watch over My sheep and* feed My flock. *Whenever they are tired*, they can lie down in the cool, *mountain grass* and rest *for as long as they like*. ¹⁶When they are lost, I will look for them and bring back every last stray. I will bind up the injured and strengthen the weak. However, I will make sure the fat and powerful *do not take advantage of the others*. I will feed them a healthy portion of judgment.

¹⁷As for you, my flock, this is what the Lord, the Eternal One says:

Eternal One

Watch carefully! I will judge between one sheep and another, between rams and goats. ¹⁸Are you not satisfied grazing in *blooming* pastures, *by feasting off rich mountain lands*? Do you have to trample all of the pastures with your feet? Are you not satisfied drinking out of clear, *pure, mountain* streams? Do you have to muddy all of the *mountain* streams with your feet? ¹⁹Why should the rest of My flock have to graze in trampled pastures and drink from muddied streams because of your *careless* feet?

²⁰Therefore, this is what the Lord, the Eternal One, says:

Eternal One

Watch carefully! I will personally judge between the fat sheep and the skinny sheep. ²¹Because you bully the weak and push them around with your haunches, shoulders, and horns until they are scattered all over *the mountains*, ²²I will step in and save them. *I will be their rescuer!* They will no longer be hunted and hassled. I will judge between one sheep and another. ²³I will designate one shepherd over the entire flock: My *faithful* servant,

David. He will *watch over them and* take care of them. He will be their shepherd. [24]I, the Eternal One, will be their True God; and My *faithful* servant, David, will be their prince. I, the Eternal One, have spoken.

One of the primary functions of the shepherd is herding. A shepherd shows his concern for the well-being of his flock by keeping them all together, regardless of each animal's whims, and moving them from pasture to pasture safely. The "shepherds" in sixth-century B.C. Jerusalem did not care about the people they led. As a result, most of God's covenant people were scattered among the pagan nations. When God spoke, those attuned to His voice heard His displeasure. They spoke His message, words of rebuke and words of hope. The Eternal One promised to become personally involved: He would bring the miserable shepherds to a miserable end, gather His chosen ones from the nations, and raise up new shepherds to lead His people. Of all the shepherds God promised, there was one Good Shepherd who would overshadow them all. The time was near, the prophets sensed, when the Liberating King, the righteous Branch of David would appear.

Jeremiah 23:1-8

Eternal One | 1 | Woe to the shepherds who slaughter and scatter My sheep!

[2]This is what the Eternal One, the True God of Israel, has to say about the shepherds tending My people:

Eternal One

You have scattered My flock, driven them far away, and failed *miserably* at being their caregivers. *In short, you've been careless, wicked leaders*; therefore, I will punish you for *your negligence*, your careless evil. ³I will personally gather the remnant of My sheep from the lands where I have driven them. I will bring them back to their home-pasture where they will be fruitful and multiply. ⁴I will appoint *new, responsible* shepherds to take care of them, and My sheep will no longer be afraid of anything. *These new, responsible shepherds will watch over every single one of My sheep and will not allow any of them* to go missing.

5 Behold! The time is near
        when I will raise up an *authentic*, righteous Branch
            of David,
        an heir of his royal line,
    A King who will rule justly and act wisely
    And bring righteousness to the land.
6 During His reign, Judah will be redeemed
        and Israel will be a safe place again.
    His name will tell the story:
        the Eternal One, our righteousness!

7 So *be ready and* watch carefully. The time is approaching, coming ever so close when no one will say any longer, "As the Eternal One lives, who freed the Israelites out of slavery in Egypt." ⁸Instead, they will say, "As the Eternal One lives, who *ended our exile* and gathered the descendants of Israel out of the north and out of all other countries where He had scattered them." Then the Israelites will live in their own land.